"There is no surety in life, only opportunity."
—Mark Twain

"Dr. Felix's memoir is a vivid reminder of how ordinary and otherwise unremarkable human beings profoundly impact us. He recounts how those in his life—people who may not be remembered by others—shaped and prepared him to be a successful leader, a university president. In this regard, *A Token of Faith* reminds me of George Eliot's beautiful reflections in *Middlemarch* about the 'daily words and acts' of 'insignificant people.' She wrote, 'the growing good of the world is partly dependent on unhistoric acts; and that things are not so ill with you and me as they might have been is half owing to the number who lived faithfully a hidden life, and rest in unvisited tombs.' That was true in Dr. Felix's life, and it is true in all of our lives."
—Dr. David Weeks, Dean of the Honors College, APU

"Richard Felix, in his candid, vulnerable, and compelling memoir, *A Token of Faith*, is replete with vivid and unexpected circumstances that defined his distinguished, visionary, and significant faith-based relational leadership in every aspect of his life. God used each unforeseen loss, frustrating unfairness, personal struggle, and pain, alongside with providing unique mentors and a myriad of successes, to shape and impact his leadership pathway. These relatable realities, in Richard's life journey, will challenge, encourage and enrich each reader, to embrace and transfer that same strength, power and confidence, to set their compass in the pursuit and purpose in their own personal life dreams." —Gordon Kirk, Th.D. Retired Senior Pastor, Member of APU Board of Trustees, and Professor of Biblical Studies

"As a trustee of APU, I had the privilege of serving as Richard's Chairman of the Board for eight of his ten years as President. For several years prior to his coming, I felt that the spiritual bulb had dimmed. Within a short time under his leadership, there was a new freedom and openness on campus that brought back the brightness to that dimmed bulb." —Dr. Don Marshburn, Former Co-Owner of Champion Seed Company and Chairman of the Board of APU (1992-2000)

A Token of Faith

RICHARD FELIX, PhD

StoryTerrace

Partial Text and Editing by Marta M. Mobley, on behalf of StoryTerrace

Design Grade Design and Adeline Media, London

First print July 2020

StoryTerrace

www.StoryTerrace.com

CONTENTS

FOREWORD

Dr. Gayle D. Beebe

President, Westmont College

From 1992-2000, I had the privilege of serving at APU under Richard's leadership. What an incredible joy and privilege. The energy and drive that infuse this book truly reflect the spirit of the man. In every way, Richard embodied a tenacious enthusiasm and relentless pursuit of excellence that` was contagious. I loved working for him and learned so many lessons about leadership and life that have guided my own twenty years as a college president. Here are five that stand out.

First, his habitual pursuit of excellence. Richard had this remarkable capacity to cast a vision and draw you into his hopes and dreams because they were so aspirational. The dreams and visions were never about him but focused on serving the greater purposes of God and the necessary improvements needed in society. I had a front-row seat as Richard, along with his beloved wife, Vivian, worked to awaken APU's latent dreams. In several sections of his book, Richard ties together the way God used others to enlarge his horizons for his own life with the way God uses others to awaken larger horizons for the institutions we lead.

Second, life can be a great teacher. Through the prism of athletics, family life, and career ambition, Richard recounts his own 'thrills of victory and agonies of defeat.' First, the haunting dissolution of his own nuclear family. Then, the love and inspiration of his life, Vivian, contracting and eventually dying from cancer. Finally, the thrill of leading two institutions only to move on, eventually retire, and learn by looking back. In each case, we're invited to explore more deeply the realities we've encountered in our own life and to discover how the shafts of God's grace and mercy actively guide our own journey.

Third, his entrepreneurial dynamism. I loved working for Richard because he was so creative and encouraged us to come up with innovative solutions as well. He wasn't afraid to try and fail, provided we were taking a pathway to a greater success. Early on, he'd learned that life often involved overcoming obstacles and setbacks. Undaunted by challenges, he believed every day was filled with possibilities, and he always directed our attention to the opportunities that lay in front of us. This infectious optimism gave him the energy, and us the confidence, to take on the Herculean task of revitalizing APU's core mission and fundamentally changing its trajectory and contribution.

Fourth, the importance of teams. Richard's own affection for athletic teams and his early professional experience as a coach gave him a deep love of identifying and developing great talent. He radiated a confidence that teams always outperform high-achieving individuals and that the sum of our efforts always exceeded the total of our individual parts. He built great executive teams during both of his presidencies. They, in turn, interfaced with the wider organization and inspired and galvanized our own interest in helping fulfill the mission. His adaptation of Drucker's mantra—bad news first, full disclosure, no surprises—brought clarity and discipline to all levels of the organization.

Finally, his endless capacity to love and invest in others. Richard's memoir reminds us that no matter what happens, we find greater meaning in what happens because of us as we respond to life's opportunities and challenges. There is every reason to imagine Richard's life turning out very different than it did. But all along the way, key individuals have redirected his steps, and Richard has been willing to take new paths as he has followed God's leading and prompting for his life. I find this so inspirational: that we can face obstacles and set-backs that should destroy us, yet somehow, through His mercy and grace, God puts people in our life who give us a sense that life could be different, better, more aligned with God's greater work in the world. Richard has found this reality and writes with this purpose. Blessings as you read.

"It is not the critic who counts; not the man who points out how the strong man stumbles, or where the doer of deeds could have done them better. The credit belongs to the man who is actually in the arena, whose face is marred by dust and sweat and blood; who strives valiantly; who errs, who comes short again and again, because there is no effort without error and shortcoming; but who does actually strive to do the deeds; who knows great enthusiasms, the great devotions; who spends himself in a worthy cause; who at the best knows in the end the triumph of high achievement, and who at the worst, if he fails, at least fails while daring greatly, so that his place shall never be with those cold and timid souls who neither know victory nor defeat."

~ Theodore Roosevelt, April 23, 1910 ~

INTRODUCTION

s a person's destiny determined by their decisions, or is it somehow chosen for them before they are born? Could it merely be a random mix of circumstances that incite us to reach our calling? There is no brief answer to this question for me, because the journey to discover my destiny was not an easy or direct one.

Many people have asked me over the years, "How did you become the president of a university?" I believe that the twenty-one years I spent as the president of two different colleges was preordained by God's direction. His teachings guided the daily choices I made that ultimately steered me down the long winding path to my destiny.

God indeed helped me to reach my vocation but also hundreds of people assisted and cheered me on along my way. This memoir shares my journey on the road to become the president of Azusa Pacific University but it is much more about their story than mine. It is my testimony to all their acts of kindness, contributions, and charity that fortified the culmination of my calling.

One such story occurred when I was eighteen years old and my church community gave me a kind token of their faith in the fall of 1957—handwritten on a small box were the words, *Helps in Higher Education*. Inside was $34.43 the members had collected for me. This much-needed money, would be my only financial aid outside of what I earned working my way through college. I still have the box today, sixty-three years later, and it holds three of the original pennies they gave me, along with pictures, photos, and news clippings I cherish. The box has always reminded me of the arduous route I began on, that inspired me to give my best to the thousands of students I taught and led, some of whom had similar difficult backgrounds to mine.

Annie Dillard, a noted writer wrote, "It takes two to ten years to write a book." I needed plenty of time since my retirement to gain the proper perspective along with much reflection about those memoirs to share my story.

This time and distance away from the decade I spent at APU provides two advantages. First, I am now free from day-to-day administrative demands and able to gain a perspective from a 10,000 feet level. I see the deeper meanings of what happened during my presidency without scrutiny or judgment. Second, I look at the university as an outsider and am able to stand in admiration of the continued progress APU has made since my retirement.

I was even more motivated to write a book about my experience at APU on the day my long-time friend, Jack DeBoer, emailed all our mutual friends and me an article from that week's Time Magazine of February 2, 2004. His words declared, "We have a famous person in our midst."

The article related the growth and prominence of faith-based colleges and universities in the country. The writer cited Azusa Pacific University for its leadership for the movement.

"In the 1990s, however, APU president Richard Felix envisioned the school as a flagship Christian university and launched its first formal fundraising program, introduced an honors program, a science research institute, created academic scholarships to lure better students, quadrupled its graduate programs and nearly doubled undergraduate enrollment, and SAT scores of freshmen within five years rose to 82 points above the national average."

The article touched and humbled me because I knew the school's history and how far we had come. Mary Hill and Mary Draper founded Azusa Pacific University in 1899 as the *Training School of Christian Workers* in Whittier. They wanted to train young men and women to respond to the social needs of that time in Los Angeles. They had Quaker roots and one of their mission outreaches each year was to Central America in which both teachers and students ministered together.

After several years of varied presidents, Cornelius Haggard took on the presidency in 1939 and held it for 36 years. The university was renamed the Pacific Bible College and offered four-year degrees. The university merged with LA Pacific College in 1965 and then Arlington College in 1968 then rechristened Azusa Pacific College. Finally, in 1981 the school was named Azusa Pacific University.

It did indeed take a few years to write my first book, but it was not the memoir you are reading now. I wrote and published the book, *The School of Dying Graces* about my beloved wife Vivian's battle with cancer. After its completion in 2004, much of my grief of her loss lessened and my heart re-opened. My children were grown, married, and blessed me with three wonderful grandchildren. Thank God I have had the time to share the stories and life lessons I write about in this book with my family and friends.

As my passion for life flourished, God provided an incredible new partner for my life. I met Susan, a lifelong educator like myself. Her love for teaching and being around children was insatiable. She is one of the kindest, loving, and most generous persons I had ever met—throwing thank-yous and kindness around like confetti. She makes others feel valued. I'm happy to share we married in a small church sanctuary in Newport Beach surrounded by our family and friends with the grandchildren playing special roles in the ceremony.

Today I live fully in the present moment with my family, friends, and expanded community. I have several outside interests and volunteer work that keeps me engaged and optimistic. Daily I express my gratitude for God's many rich blessings. I choose not to live in the past, but writing this memoir has been a pleasant and insightful walk down memory lane and I believe its publication will be one of God's final assignments for me.

I sincerely hope my story and life lessons give the reader a token of faith in humanity just as I was given and they will be inspired to discover the essential cornerstones we created for Azusa Pacific University: Christ, Community, Scholarship, and Service.

PART ONE
A COMMITMENT TO CHRIST

1

A FORMIDABLE INFANCY

"Character building begins in our infancy and continues until our death."

~Eleanor Roosevelt~

G od must have had a plan when he brought me into this world on October 17, 1938 in Lafayette, Indiana and bestowed me to two lost teenagers who at first found comfort in each other's arms, then only hatred. It was never their intention to have a baby or get married to each other.

My father, Frances "Bud" Felix was a nomadic construction worker who had grown up working on his family's farm under the firm hand of his father. The last thing he wanted when he was free to escape his laborious upbringing was more grueling responsibility. His family forced them into their ill-fated vows. He was angry from the moment he found out my mother was pregnant and despised his new role as husband and father. His resentment grew during their marriage and they fought often, moving from place to place with their unwanted baby, then toddler, barely struggling for their survival.

My mother was in high school and suddenly went from taking care of her father and five brothers, to a life on the road with an aggrieved husband and malnourished child. Her mother had died when she was only one-year-old and it became clear after my birth that she did not understand how to be a mother.

I was only five years old when my world turned upside down forever. This moment happened during the middle of an especially dark, yet peaceful winter night. I was fast asleep when I abruptly awakened, then terrified by the sound of my mother screaming. Suddenly my father appeared at the foot of my bed. She rushed towards him crying. He grabbed me by my arms while she desperately tried her best to pull him away from me.

"No, no...please leave the little boy alone. He is not the cause of our troubles!" He dropped me back onto the bed and threw her to the floor like a rag doll, then towered over me with wrath in his eyes. She pulled herself to her knees and tried to recover. She struggled to reach out her arms to protect me, but he kicked her back to the floor.

"You are nothing but problems for us!" He shouted and dragged me out of the bed. My mother grasped for me, but he shoved her aside and carried me clutched under his arm to the apartment door. He pushed me outside and onto the apartment landing into the bitter night air as if I were a bag of garbage. "Get out of here and never come back or I'll kill you."

"No daddy, I don't want to go. I love you." I cried and reached my arms out towards him, repeatedly pleading the same words.

My mother appeared at the door and tried her best to extend her arms to me, but he lurched towards me and blocked her from getting out the door. Then my mother squeezed by him and finally escaped outside to rescue me. She scooped me up in her arms, ran down the stairs while somehow she wrapped me up in a blanket.

She hurried down the street as I heard my father's hateful words echoing in my head. "I'll kill you!" I did not understand. Why did he hate me? Why didn't he love and want me?

She carried me in the freezing cold three blocks down the street to a place we knew well. It was midnight when she desperately knocked, and my paternal grandmother opened the door. "The only safe place for him is here," my mother said and handed me into my grandmother's arms.

I have no doubt my grandmother repeated silent prayers under her breath as she laid me on the sofa and sat close by my side to comfort my frightened soul until I fell asleep.

I would never spend another night with my parents again for the rest of my life. Later, they divorced and I would only see my mother one more time when I reached adulthood. I would spend decades trying to gather and repair the pieces of my broken heart after that painful winter night in Indiana.

Despite being poor, my grandparents loved me beyond measure. When they lost their farm during the Great Depression, my elderly grandfather went to work in a factory building prefab homes to support our family. My bedroom was upstairs and my two aunts shared an adjoining room while my grandparents slept in the living room. We all shared one tiny bathroom. I had one pair of tattered jeans and a well-worn white shirt that became my daily uniform.

My grandfather was a wise father, a tough taskmaster in running the family farm. He took pride in his work and could get the job done, no matter how difficult the circumstances. The Peloquin Dit Felix Credy family grew from three generations of French Québécois who emigrated from France in the 1600s. They were a society dominated by religion, proud of their ancestry and hard-work ethic. He was kind and deferential to what my grandmother wanted or needed. Obviously he loved her very much despite their years of hardship together.

My grandmother Grace was an angel on earth and would become my protector. She provided me with an abundant supply of internal gifts, which helped me flourish. It was ironic that this woman was the mother of the man who left his child feeling unwanted and abandoned.

Even though we lived in poverty, my grandmother's spirit brought riches into my heart. She modeled the art of being resilient through her daily actions. When our nation was deeply involved in World War II, her youngest son was seriously injured on the war front. His captors transported him along with hundreds of other injured and deceased soldiers in huge boxcars to hospitals towards the end of the war. At night I remember her praying and crying out with a broken heart to God for his safety. Her sobbing permeated our little home, but the deafening message was that her faith in God was strong.

Her generosity was abundant. She cared for others less fortunate in our church. She brought baked goods and dropped extra dollars on the offering plate even though we were skimping on rations at home. With the two storms of poverty and war constantly swirling around us, she praised the Lord again and again.

Her natural optimism and joyfulness during this time of difficulty became rooted in my DNA. I likely inherited this ability or curse from her. Sometimes it served me to be an idealist in my behavior when I faced hard times. But on other occasions, it was detrimental because it blinded me to other's faults and misdeeds.

She taught me humility and influenced my spiritual life. We attended church twice on Sunday and a prayer meeting during the week. Her authenticity and devotion as a follower of Christ inspired me to be just like her when I grew up. She was emotional in her prayers during worship in church and shed tears of joy as she called out the name of Jesus. Sitting next to her in church, I observed her every action. She loved to sing the Fanny Crosby hymns as she revealed both her pleasure and pain, sometimes joined with laughter. Her damp handkerchiefs were a testimony to her passion.

I learned to love Jesus and to be resilient at the feet of my grandmother. The Bible was always open in our home. We would read from it in the morning and at night before retiring to bed. Memorizing scripture was part of our routine. At bedtime she taught me to pray with my eyes closed and try to imagine Jesus right beside me. "Imagine his arms are wide open to receive you." She directed me to voice my prayer out loud and then she would wrap her loving arms around me to reassure me.

Sometimes I would cry for my dad and she reminded me I had a heavenly father and His son's name was Jesus. She assured me as I grew older, I would learn to connect with him at Sunday school and church and at twelve years of age, I could give my heart and life to Him if I wished.

She was right. Jesus would be an even greater savior to me than my real father on earth. When I was twelve years old, I accepted Jesus as my Lord and Savior. "I am the way, the truth, and the life: no man comes unto the Father but by me." (John 14:6)

My grandmother understood my needs as a young boy. She believed besides having a relationship with my heavenly father, I needed to have fun and experience the joys of friendship. She occasionally allowed me to go with the neighborhood boys to Saturday morning movie serials at a local movie theater. I appreciate now how God's plan served me, and how I thrived being raised under the care of my grandmother. When our difficult life experiences are seen through the eyes of a child, it is hard to heal a broken heart because the pain is still so close in sight.

Thankfully one of the gifts of age is that we are eventually able to reflect on the past with a clearer perspective. I understand now my parents' lives were complicated tremendously by poverty. Their problems were in part born of circumstances they couldn't control and I was not the reason for their troubles. I learned that God makes all things beautiful in his time. And, most of all, I am grateful for the turn of fate in my childhood, because it provided me with the greatest blessing of all, my wonderful and Godly Grandmother, Grace Penrod Felix who became the first savior in my life.

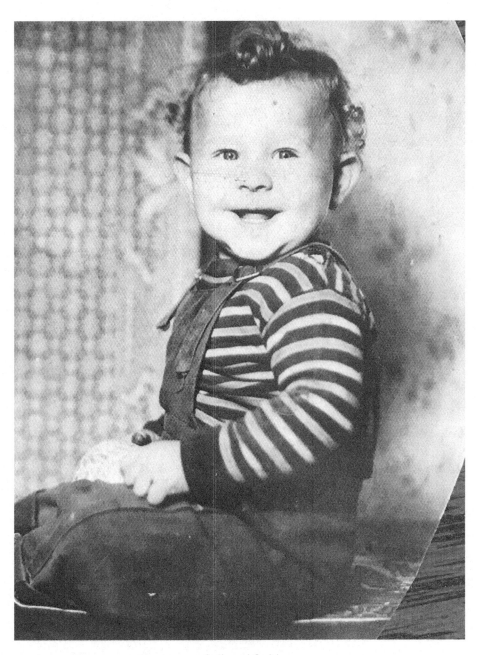

Smiles and Curls!

With Grandma Grace

Grandparents, Grace and Charles Felix

2

BLESSED IN MIDDLE CHILDHOOD

"You were made by God and for God, and until you understand that, life will never make sense."

~ Rick Warren ~

My grandparents' house was located on the corner of Greenbush and 15th Streets. My bedroom was about the size of a large closet and sparsely furnished. My window was positioned directly across the street from my elementary school on one side and an empty field on the other. When I looked out, I could see grassy expanses of fields in the milder months and a snowy wonderland in winter. In the summer, the enticing smell of the grass and eucalyptus trees was a calling card I could never ignore. No ticket needed as I dashed outside to explore.

My passion for sports began at a young age. Baseball, basketball, football, or whatever the season, I was game. The warm evenings offered the neighborhood kids impromptu baseball games. From my bedroom window I perched and waited until I saw the kids run down the street through the surrounding bushes and brush to meet on the field. My heart pounding, I'd grab my mitt and run out the front door to meet Donny, Huey, the Dent brothers, Jerry, Charlie, Bernie. Most of us had a mitt but someone would bring a makeshift bat and our balls were old worn used baseballs wrapped in black tape. In reflection, it must have looked like a scene from the 1989 movie *Field of Dreams*. We had created our own neighborhood team.

The Wednesday night basketball games at our local high school were also a high priority. Two of my buddies and I would always occupy the front row near the scorers' bench for every game. We knew each player and everything about their stats. Unfortunately, Wednesday was also prayer meeting night at our church. Some church elders expressed displeasure at what they thought was sinful behavior on my part and lack of control by my grandmother. She politely explained that there was nothing sinful about basketball. Our pastor saw what was happening and stepped in on our behalf to referee the call. At the end of the match, the pastor came to my defense and we won.

As my interest in baseball intensified, I read a multitude of books from our local library and devoured newspapers and magazines on the topic. A 20-something year old man named Leroy lived a few houses down the street. While he was home nursing his war injuries, he enhanced my baseball education through his subscription of Al Spink's *The Sporting News*. It was founded in 1896 and was unofficially called the Bible of Baseball. Leroy got his first copy of the newspaper overseas where it was distributed free to all servicemen.

Each week as I sat by his bedside, he spoke with excitement about the players from the 1930's and 1940's and always gave me his magazine when he was finished. As is typical of those great men of his generation, he never spoke of WWII. Baseball was our common bond. As passion morphed into obsession, I decided to start my baseball card collection. After I began collecting, my evening ritual after dinner was always the same. "Grandma, may I be excused from the table?" As soon as she said yes, I bounded up the stairs and slid across the top of my bed just like a runner sliding to home plate. Safe!

I eagerly searched for the lidless shoebox under my bed. With breakneck speed, my well-practiced fingers stretched a piece of string into a baseball diamond and placed markers for the bases, the fields and catcher's box. The cigar box dugouts were filled with baseball cards of the individual players and a spitball was placed on the pitcher's mound. Then I'd peel a clump of last night's bubble gum from the rail on my bed, toss it in my mouth and exclaim, "It's a beautiful day for baseball at Wrigley Field!"

In my imaginary field, I was the manager, announcer, scorekeeper and statistician. The locker room speech each night would include fighting words, "C'mon guys! The dreaded Cardinals are in town today! Give it your best!"

Announcing each play for the invisible fans in my room was fun. "Ernie Banks is in the batter's box, he swings and there is a long drive into deep left field, the left fielder drifts back towards the ivy-covered wall, it's over his head and onto Waveland Avenue, home run!" I recorded each play on the scoreboard, moved each baseball card player to his next place on the field or dugout and kept all the stats. At age nine my leadership and multi-tasking skills were emerging already.

You might say that I received the equivalent to a PhD in Baseball through baseball cards. It wasn't a very expensive degree. You could get a pack of cards for ten cents. Not only did I learn how to compute earned run and batting averages, I also studied the Mason-Dixon line's influence on the sport, which fed my curiosity to learn more about our country's history. The entire education curriculum I fondly christened SHOE BOX 101.

The following day goes down in baseball history as one of the happiest days of my life. I was ten years old walking pensively home from school. I noticed a sign on the gate that read: Little League Baseball - Tryouts TODAY! Ages 10-12. I peered through the wire fence at the baseball field still rock hard from the winter snow where a group of taller and older boys gathered at home plate in circle formation around the coach.

I shrugged my shoulders and pulled my cap over my eyes as I dug my hand in my pocket to pull out a baseball card. It was my most prized card - Babe Ruth. He seemed to be smiling at me. "Hey, kid! Trying out for the team?" the coach called out to me. My head nodded before I could think, and my feet shuffled towards the team as if my legs were being pulled by an invisible string dragging my body across third base and onto home plate.

A couple of kids turned and smirked at me. One muttered, "Hey, Squirt!" as I approached the boys. I learned that they were twelve year olds and had played on the team last year. During the next hour I plowed through like a mighty giant as we ran drills, fielded balls, and took some batting practice. At the end of the tryout, my name was added to the list of kids who made the cut. I smiled all the way home, just like Babe did after hitting a home run.

Fully fortified by this Little League experience, my next step forward was joining the Pony League at the age of thirteen. At the end of the season, they selected me for the All-Star Team that would play in the state tournament, a day permanently embedded in my memory.

The score was tied towards the end of the game and it was my turn at bat. Right before I took the batter's box, Coach Jack Hopkins called me over and said, "This guy throws mostly fast balls. Watch out! Be ready!"

Driven by a mission, I walked to home base, tapped the plate with my bat, and took a few practice swings. I focused my eyes on the pitcher with a laser stare. The pitch came at me and I swung. The sound of the bat contact and crowd cheering told me I had made good. As I rounded first base, I noticed the outfielders looking around for the ball and saw it was beyond the fence. I had hit the game-winning home run.

As I rounded third base, the coach rushed out and knocked my hat off in congratulations. When I reached home plate, I became lost in the arms of my screaming team-mates and eventually ended up being smothered at the bottom of the pile. Gasping for breath and wiping dirt from my face, I felt an overwhelming sense of pride and worth. After the game, the coach singled me out and commended me for being an invaluable part of the team. Jack Hopkins would become another one of God's angels in my life.

Childhood Home

Dreaming about Baseball

Linnwood Elementary School
(front row, fourth from left)

3

AWAKENING IN ADOLESCENCE

"Get all the advice and instruction you can, so you will be wise the rest of your life."

~ Proverbs 19:20 ~

On the first day of high school I strode into my freshman composition class and stopped short when I saw the teacher. It was Jack Hopkins. I said, "Hi Coach!" and sat down with a determination to please him as a scholar the same way I had as an athlete. He believed in me and was a strong male role model I desperately needed.

As it turned out, his mentorship helped me get through the complicated years of high school. Even though I was physically fit and excelled at sports, I still had a lot of self worth issues in my high school years. I also had lingering uncertainties about my father not wanting me and was self-conscious about smiling.

I grew up with missing and discolored teeth. As a child, I often cried at night because my mouth was in so much pain. My grandmother would come into my room and kneel by my bed. She would dab alcohol on a cotton swab and ask me to hold it on my tooth to numb the throbbing. "I'm so sorry, Dick," she often said. "We just can't afford to take you to the dentist. Oh, how I wish. . . I wish," she stammered and regarded me with grief-stricken eyes.

I knew what she wanted to say. I'd heard it many times before from various family members. "I wish his parents hadn't neglected him as a baby with a poor diet and given him the wrong formula. I wish he had the proper medical care."

No one wished it more than me. When talking to other people, I developed the fine art of balancing my hand under my nose to shield my teeth. When girls tried to talk to me in the hallway, I would keep walking and pretend not to hear them. My defensive actions to hide my teeth were my modus operandi for years. I had become two people in one body. The man inside was outgoing, humorous and loved by his friends. But the embarrassed part of me hid from the world because he could not smile.

With or without a smile, resilience grew throughout these years. I learned that life was a series of valleys and mountaintops, deep ravines and towering peaks. My role models exhibited how to be joyful and optimistic in the face of adversity. I observed my grandfather limp in the backdoor of our kitchen after a hard day's work and still be up early the next day to do it all over again.

My grandmother kept her faith and support of me despite her aging and having already raised her own children, yet still had room in her heart for a poor unwanted child like me. Through all the ups and downs of high school, I learned to move forward in devotion and trust that God's words would guide my way.

Another key angel who influenced the course of my life was my church pastor, Reverend Kenneth Foust. Our youth group all knew he loved us because he frequently joined us playing basketball and baseball and drove us to church camp each summer. There were four of us from the Lafayette Church of the Nazarene who came from broken families and he encouraged us to attend a Christian college. I was deeply touched by his encouraging spirit when he actually drove me to Olivet Nazarene University in Bourbonnais, Illinois to help me enroll for my first classes.

At the last Sunday service before I left for college, Reverend Foust gave an inspired sermon to send us off to school. When church ended, the pastor called me to the altar and handed me a cigar box inscribed with the words *Helps in Higher Education*. I opened it and discovered $34.43 in cash. To my surprise and elation, our congregation had gathered a collection to invest in my future. Deeply humbled by this token of faith, I vowed to repay their trust by making a difference with my life.

Lafayette Jefferson High School Graduation

The Token Box
63 years later

With grandparents at graduation

PART TWO
A COMMITMENT TO COMMUNITY

4

POTENTIAL IN EARLY ADULTHOOD

"It is in your moment of decision that your destiny is determined."

~ Tony Robbins ~

owed it to my role models and myself to be the best version of Richard Felix I could be. The summer before I began college, I got a job working in construction and making a good wage. I had more confidence and wanted to take action to fully express the real me. I met with a local dentist to determine how much it would cost to have my teeth repaired. We set a timeline, which allowed me to save enough money to have the extensive procedure completed by fall. I worked harder than I ever had driven by a determination to change my life. The entire process took over a month.

I had to skip the fall college semester to earn enough money to pay for both the dental work and the upcoming tuition in January. I was over-the-moon when the dentist gave me the mirror to see the real me for the first time. I studied my face with intention and gratitude. With the possession of a new radiant smile, I was empowered to begin the next part of my journey.

I must own that my first two years at Olivet were not my best in terms of academic achievement. At the end of my sophomore year, just before heading home for the summer, I stopped by Professor Harvey Humble's office to check my final grade in his history class.

"Mr. Felix, come into my office and sit down," he said as he pulled his chair closer to mine and peered intently at my face. "You are an enigma to me. You are settling for C's in my class, yet I noticed you are best friends with my two top students. I don't think they would hang out with you if you were a dummy."

My bright smile faded into a frown as his words sunk deep into my heart. He leaned forward with a definite grin showing through his trademark black mustache. "Why don't you return in the fall and take my Civil War and Reconstruction class? I think you could be one of my top students if you applied yourself." His stinging words and challenge gave me a great deal to think about.

That summer back in Lafayette, I worked for a subcontractor on a major road project near Purdue University. I led a team of four men in pouring and finishing a special curbing. One day the Superintendent of the entire project approached me. "My people and I have noticed you. We like your work ethic and ability to get along with our key personnel. I'd like to offer you a full-time job traveling with us all over the nation. Our company will supply all the tools and equipment to do your work. The man who used to do this work for us has retired."

I paused to steady my spinning head, and finally managed to stutter out a few words, "Well, um...I'd have to give it some thought because I'm planning to return to college this fall."

"OK, think it over. I'm around all the time if you have any questions. He turned to walk away and then pivoted back to say, "Oh, by the way, your earnings would be about forty thousand dollars a year. Let me know what you decide." I inhaled a gulp of air and replied, "Well, sure, thanks.'

The money was a great temptation and I agonized over the decision for the next couple of weeks. I could really help my grandparents with that kind of salary. It was a difficult and pivotal moment in my life. Did I want to be a scholar or work in construction for the rest of my life? But what about the amazing offer to travel all over the country?

One Sunday evening in early August, Reverend Foust's sermon focused on living a life of service. "We all face choices in life. The Bible is full of examples of both good and bad choices. The scripture again and again tells us to choose a life that lives for something bigger than ourselves. Too many older people later in life regret not choosing a life of service to others."

I thought about my pastor's eloquent words and reflected seriously about my future plans as I continued working on my summer job. Every day I watched and heard the talking and laughter from the Purdue students as they walked to classes. They were animated in conversations and glimmers of dreams to be chased glowed in their eyes. I saw the confidence in their steps.

Gradually, after a couple of weeks a desire for the passion and purpose they exhibited planted a firm decision in my heart. I needed to complete my college education. With this one determined decision, I accepted Harvey Humble's challenge. I returned to classes in the fall and received an A grade in my Civil War and Reconstruction class. I became a lifelong scholar.

Financing college expenses was still a critical challenge despite my church's token of faith money and my summer construction work salary, so I accepted a job during my junior and senior years as the District Circulation Manager for a Chicagoland newspaper. Since it was only a few afternoons a week and all day Saturday, I was certain I could balance my studies and a new job.

My responsibilities included recruiting, hiring, and training 100 paper boys/girls aged 12-16. My goal was to instill in them a strong work ethic, commitment to their customers, importance of on-time delivery and weekly collections. Since my territory included 40 square miles the task was not an easy one. On some days I would have to deliver papers a child neglected or have a heart-to-heart talk with a struggling parent. Despite the inherent stress, I loved working with the children and families.

At my graduation two years later it felt as if I was receiving two degrees: one from Olivet and one from the School of Hard Knocks. The liberal arts education was invaluable because it provided a wide perspective of knowledge that would enhance the rest of my life. My work experience was similarly significant in that it had added leadership skills to my repertoire and a unique collection of essential life lessons.

My post-college goals were threefold: discover a mission to guide my life, find a soul mate to complement the journey God had planned for me, and pursue a career of service that would reflect my mission and passion in life.

For the next three years, I continued my newspaper position along with working in the public schools and completing a master's degree in Chicago at George Williams College, now Aurora University. It became clear I was a gifted multi-tasker and felt energized in the process. After a year serving as the fifth grade teacher of an elementary school in Illinois, the school administration catapulted me into the role of principal the next year. I felt a little nervous about the new position because most of the teachers were old enough to be my mother.

Sometimes we learn the most from those we were hired to lead, and this was one of those situations. As I chaired my first faculty meeting, I listened as the veteran teachers recognized student's needs, and patiently made difficult decisions to stimulate improvement in effort and determination. What I learned about building community and the administration of tough love from these wonderful mentors was essential for my future positions. It appeared that God had the dynamic duo of young people and education in his plans for me.

Then on a magical day in the summer of 1964, I saw my soon to be wife for the first time. I remember falling under the spell of her beauty from a baseball field where I stood manned on first base. I was playing for my church softball team and noticed a blue convertible pull up into the parking lot alongside our team's bleachers. I remember gazing at her as I tried to focus on what was going on in the game.

After we finished, I made it a point to tell my teammate Don, who was standing next to this beautiful girl, how well he played. "Thanks!" he said, "Oh, by the way, this is my wife Millie and sister-in-law Vivian." I smiled, and then stammered a few words to her. I can still recall the way her green eyes caught the light of the afternoon sun.

As soon as I got home, I grabbed a copy of that year's Olivet yearbook. I paged back through the seniors, the juniors, the sophomores, and finally to the freshmen. My fingers traced the names until I came across a picture of Vivian Stray. I still vividly recollect my decision to ask her out on a date. Determined to meet her again, I decided at that moment to drive to Olivet where Vivian was a sophomore. I drove around the campus hoping I would accidentally run into her.

On my second pass, I saw her walking near the library with some of her friends through my rearview mirror. Unfortunately, it was a one-way street. I sped up the road, turned around, but by the time I made it back to the spot where I had seen her, she disappeared.

I was so disappointed that when I returned home; I summoned the courage to call her and was surprised she picked up. "Hello Vivian, my name is Richard Felix. You probably don't remember me, but I played first base at one of your brother-in-law's softball games last summer." I swallowed so hard that I was sure she had heard my gulp.

"Oh I know who you are," she responded with a laugh. "You're the guy who forgot your shoes and drove away from the game barefooted!" She laughed and we chatted, then eventually I got to my point. "Could I take you to church next week? And maybe we could get a bite after?" I asked. Thankfully, she replied, "Sure." After we hung up, I ran around my house shouting repeatedly, "She's so beautiful!"

Almost immediately, I knew I wanted and needed Vivian in my life. In her presence I had a sense of completion and she soon felt the same way about me. I found her exotic Asian beauty mesmerizing. She was the daughter of a Chinese doctor and an American missionary, and had grown up in a wonderful family with an abundance of love, care, and support. All invaluable gifts I coveted, of which I had never received from my parents.

Marrying into Vivian's family was an absolute blessing in every way. Her parents, David and Mildred Stray, and her sister Millie, were very affectionate, kind, and accepting of me from the moment we met. After we married, we had dinner with them every chance we could. They invested in me emotionally, spiritually, and later financially.

Dr. Stray expressed confidence in me that had been lacking from my own father. I continue to thank God daily for His blessings and goodness with this divine plan for my life. I had finally found a family and community that provided me healing at so many levels.

It seemed natural for us to start a family after we married. That day would change the direction of my life forever. On the day of my first child's birth, I sat both nervous and scared in the waiting room when a smiling nurse appeared from the maternity ward carrying a baby wrapped in a blue blanket. "Mr. Felix, this is your precious newborn son." A rush of emotions bubbled up in my chest as she cradled him into my arms. This was a sacred moment in my life.

At first I was speechless as my eyes surveyed the tiny features of his face, his dark eyes and hair. "He is sure to be a tall boy based on his birth length," she said. I looked up at her teary eyed and with a big smile, "I can't wait to shoot baskets in the driveway and throw a football in the backyard," I said.

I gazed down at his sweet face. Most importantly, I wanted to teach him to love God and to always be himself. I took a deep breath and reflected over my own tough childhood. I could still recall overhearing relatives say, "Dick will grow up to be just like his father." This had fueled a fire in me that still burned, and I knew right then that I would be nothing like him.

I looked at Doak David in my arms and thanked God for giving me a son that I could love and cherish. I made a promise to him I would be a supportive and caring father every day of his life.

As I look back over those years, I realized I was a fortunate man to have achieved all three of my post college goals before I was thirty years old. I became a blessed husband to my soul mate Vivian and over the next few years became the father of two more wonderful children, Tristram Earl and Melissa Elizabeth. The students I taught educated me in the important mission their teachers played in encouraging them to learn, grow, and succeed. I was now working in a career of service that I was very passionate about helping to build a community that had eternal value.

Wedding with Vivian

5

ENTERPRISE IN ADULTHOOD

"The secret is to work less as individuals and more as a team. As a coach, I play not my eleven best, but my best eleven."

~ Knute Rockne ~

I n 1967, Dr. Norman Bridges, Dean of Students at Bethel College in Indiana offered me a job as the Athletic Director and Head Basketball Coach. This assignment surpassed my dream of someday becoming a high school coach. The world of higher education was like stepping out into deep water and I dived right in. Since sports can often be the ultimate laboratory for learning about leadership and teamwork, I was now in an arena of high-intensity growth.

At twenty-eight years old, I was not much older than my players. I enjoyed joining scrimmage games with them and encouraged their development as athletes and individuals. Most importantly, I had a front-row seat watching them grow together, respecting and trusting each other, and building a deep sense of individual worth and community value.

When I began coaching, I remembered a time back in 1950 when my Aunt Maxine and Uncle Gilbert took me to a Cubs vs. Dodgers game at Wrigley Field in Chicago. I sat in awe as Jackie Robinson stole two or three bases, much to the delight of the most die-hard Cub fans. I said, "Uncle Gilbert, I don't understand why the Cub fans are cheering." He explained, "Jackie is the first African American to play in the major leagues and he might even be the best player in all of baseball. His base stealing is exciting and electric, even if you're a Cub fan."

After that game, I immediately began collecting, saving and trading my friends for Jackie's cards. I loved his story of overcoming incredible obstacles to make it to the major leagues. As I took on this new assignment at Bethel College, one of my greatest privileges was recruiting the first African American student athletes in that school's history.

These students were a positive influence not only on the basketball court but across campus academically and socially. It was a satisfying experience, at a time when racial relations across America were still unsettled in the late 1960s.

Perhaps our most memorable moment together occurred when we won the championship game at a holiday tournament in Ohio. It was the first championship in the school's history for basketball or any sport. When we returned to the locker room, everyone celebrated by dousing me with water. Following dinner the whole team, including managers literally piled into my tiny hotel room to continue the merriment—loud, noisy, and disorderly.

They kept recalling the special moments and critical plays of the game, taking pictures with the trophy, and replaying the game winning shot just before the clock expired. You could cut that sense of joy and community with a knife.

They recognized the team the following Monday morning in Bethel Chapel. The applause was enthusiastic and deafening. Winning is important, but even better is the understanding that the team gives its best, lives up to its collective potential and is respectful and trusting of each other.

Fast-forward fifty-three years to 2016, many players, including some from this first team, gathered once again for a special ceremony in their honor at a Bethel Basketball game. Since the original banner hanging in the gym had disintegrated, they replaced it with a newly designed one with students, staff, alumni, media, in attendance. Older and wiser, my team was still on the court surrounded by our community.

During the time at Bethel our family grew, but my salary did not. Our Bethel income was only five thousand dollars per year, which is a fraction of what we had earned in Illinois. Our family was living close to the poverty line, so I signed up to teach two summer classes at the college. I taught one class to local high school teachers who wanted to be State certified to teach driver education. The capstone was that each teacher had to teach a 16-year-old how to drive. Over a hundred teenage applicants applied to be one of the twelve guinea pigs for this opportunity.

I soon realized there were more than a hundred students who we couldn't accommodate. I scribbled some ideas down and created a business plan. I negotiated to use the college's driver's education car and acquired state certification. I thought, why don't I open up a school for driver's education?

The challenge of starting my business from scratch was daunting and sadly took a lot of time away from my family. I quickly learned to navigate the issues of state certification. I learned to assess the marketplace and how to reach both students and potential instructors. As business prospered, I had to learn to purchase and finance additional cars, buy equipment, negotiate insurance, and service the automobiles. It was difficult and took a lot of gumption with hard work.

After a year, we were doing so well; I rented an office on the college campus, hired secretarial help to field phone calls, make appointments, schedule drivers, meet payroll, and grade tests. Through this process, we eventually added five more cars to our fleet and our profit soared to fifteen thousand dollars a year.

I remember sitting at the dinner table one evening with Vivian. "We don't have to skimp anymore. The driving school's success will allow us to do some things with the kids. Some new clothes for you and the children." She smiled sadly and replied, "That's wonderful Richard, but we really miss you and only want more time with you."

I wish now, looking back at her openness that I had taken to heart what she and the kids wanted. But I felt compelled to provide a better life for my family; no matter how hard I had to work or time it took.

November 11, 1967 was one of the saddest days of my life. My grandmother Grace passed away. Her graduation and ascension to God was traumatic for me, and my family as well. Grandma was the kinkeeper of the Felix clan. Her loving spirit of kindness was bestowed equally to her church family, neighbors, my elementary teachers, her adult children, and her grandchildren. Over the years her wisdom would indeed be true and she would live up to her name, Grace.

She was so proud of me. It was almost embarrassing. I remember her telling people that I earned a college degree and was a teacher at a university. She loved and spent a lot of time with Vivian and her great grandchild, little Doak.

Her funeral was packed with people. The pastor gave a sermon and our family eulogized her. A movie of my life began to play in my head. I couldn't stop the tears flowing as I recalled the hundreds of instances she rescued my wounded soul as a child. As I looked around the church, I realized that many others had been touched by her loving essence. Several in attendance remarked how much Grandma had been the mother that they never had.

Professionally, I had become a new empowered version of myself. I enjoyed the freedom of creating something from nothing. I relished the fact I had taken a dream scribbled on a piece of notepaper and turned it into a profitable business. I couldn't believe the independence that one idea had given our family financial stability, but did not realize at what cost and sacrifice.

Finally, I learned the tremendous responsibility and loneliness that comes with being the leader of a business enterprise. The reality of leadership sank in and I realized profits weren't everything. But life was going well. We were happy monetarily and then it hit me; I wanted more. It seemed the right time to invest in becoming more mature in my faith and my mission to become a leader.

After sharing thoughts with several of my colleagues, they suggested I look into a way to complete a doctorate. Each of them had found time to do so. They opined that the success of my driving school would allow my family the financial support so it would be possible to complete the degree. Shortly thereafter, Notre Dame accepted me into the PhD program in Higher Education. To allow time for this venture, my cousin Gib Young agreed to assist with the driving school.

When I told my wife I wanted to go back to school to get my doctorate, she patiently smiled and restated the same request as before. "That's great Richard, but what we really want is more time with you. When you finish your doctorate, I want our family to live a normal family life again."

Basketball Team at Bethel College

The Coach in Action

Basketball Team 50 years later

6

A NEW PASSION IN MIDLIFE

"And we know that God causes everything to work together for the good of those who love God and are called according to His purpose for them."

~ Romans 8:28 ~

When I arrived at Notre Dame, it was love at first sight. The campus emanated rich history and architecture. It had a spirit of place that transcended any of the major state universities I had visited. My professors were all scholars—tough and demanding—yet with a spiritual side that struck me as refreshing.

I worked full time on a PhD while overseeing my business. To be honest, I was not there for my family as much as I wanted. Some nights I arrived home late and my children were fast asleep. Too many mornings I was up before my family to begin another busy day. I rationalized working on the degree and having a business for my family's well-being and future.

During this time, I was blessed to have such an amazing wife to take on the heavy load of raising our children. She taught them to love God and instilled the values of family togetherness. Little did I realize that by default, I had brought my family into a life of service and they sacrificed so I could learn.

Despite my busy schedule, I had breakfast and dinner with my family most days. My fondest memories were of playing games and wrestling on the floor with my children. We had one game called Billy Goats Gruff, which we played almost every night when the kids were aged four to seven. Of course, reading them stories and praying with them before bedtime became one of the most sacred times for our family.

A poignant *God moment* occurred during that first year of classes. It was a frigid evening as I left my class in the Golden Dome of Notre Dame and sloshed my way through the snow to the Basilica of the Sacred Heart. The door cracked open and the candlelight from the interior beckoned me inside. I had enrolled in a three-year PhD program and my plate was full. My weary body fell onto the prayer bench and my shivering lips told God what He already knew.

Dear Lord - I have been juggling my positions with starting a business, caring for my wife and three children and attending classes at Notre Dame. Am I doing too much? Am I living out your purpose? You have given me so much. How might my life and skills be used to serve a deeper purpose? Please, dear God, hear my prayer and be my shepherd, I am your lamb. Amen.

I sat in solitude and felt a halo of warmth that surrounded me before I left. It filled my heart and soul with gratitude to continue my education and experience varied opportunities. Renewed faith and confidence in this moment encouraged me to move forward. Faith gave me the assurance that God would give me the strength and opportunity to use my talents as a multi-tasker.

On my way back to my car, I remember looking up to the brightly lit-window where Father Hesburgh, the much-loved President of Notre Dame, was still working in his office. Another light turned on inside me and I asked, *Is it possible I could be a university president one day? Was this part of God's plan that led me here?* At this moment a divine seed was planted inside me and I would carry the vision of a university president as my mission in life.

As the time came near to my completion of the PhD program, Vivian and I spent considerable time contemplating our future. One afternoon we took a break away to a nearby park and had a picnic. I shared, "You know, as financially wonderful as the driving school has become, it's not our true calling." She agreed but confessed, "I have been a little depressed during these cold, miserable Midwest winters because the kids and I rarely leave the house. Maybe now when you complete your doctorate, whatever that true calling is, we could follow it to a warmer climate?"

We agreed we wanted to move, and both acknowledged that our mission was to serve in Christian higher education. As it happened, a few months later, Trevecca Nazarene College invited me to become a Vice President of Advancement. It was a wonderful Christian college in Nashville, Tennessee. Coincidentally, our dear college friends, Ed and Judy Nash, were pastoring the College Hill Church on campus.

I learned a great deal from my years at Trevecca and our family adjusted to our life in the southern belt of our country. I was blessed to have more traditional work hours. This allowed me to spend evenings and weekends with our family enabling me to coach Tris' youth basketball team and for Vivian to complete her Masters Degree at Middle Tennessee State University.

In the summer of 1978, I was accepted into a Post Doctoral program at Harvard Business School. Every year they admitted one hundred young leaders to spend six days a week for six weeks being tutored in the finer issues of higher education. The faculty also included leaders in business, medicine, and education from across the United States.

The program turned out to be rigorous. During our class sessions we would have to defend our position on a particular case study. The faculty, the other students and the author of the case study drilled us with questions for an hour. They challenged our assumptions, values, and positions. I was blessed to be accepted into the program, but it meant being in Boston away from my family.

At the end of the class sessions, I realized I could compete with other aspiring leaders and hold my own with people of high caliber academic credentials. Not only was my sense of self worth affirmed, but I felt empowered to be a college president. This was God's way of confirming that calling.

Upon returning to Nashville, The University of Florida offered me the Director of Major Gifts position. At forty-years-old, I leapt at the chance to learn more about how a university Major Gifts program worked.

After serving only one year in my position, I received a phone call that once again would change my life forever. I shook my head in disbelief as I hung up the phone. Vivian shouted from the living room, 'What was that all about?" I yelled back, "It was the chairman of the presidential search committee at Friends University. I have been nominated for their presidency."

She walked into the kitchen with a furrowed brow and questioning eyes. "Where in the world is Friends University?" She looked hopeful. "Wichita, Kansas," I replied. She slumped her shoulders and asked, "Isn't it cold there like Indiana?"

Our heads and hearts got caught in an ocean of turbulent waves of "what ifs?" We had just moved our family to Gainesville, Florida and were just getting settled. I loved my new position and was gaining invaluable experience. Vivian was taking classes at the University, enjoying some newfound freedom, and doing some writing. We established the kids at their new schools, and we were all enjoying the warm weather.

"Vivian, it's too soon to even think about another move." She agreed, and we thought we finished the discussion. Then we received a call from our former colleagues, Fred and Marti Garlett, who had nominated us. During several phone calls, their enthusiasm about the school and faculty was infectious. They shared how nice it was to be in a community that offered a smaller environment and a slower pace.

They were so convincing that we reconsidered the offer and forwarded my resume to the university. Then the Chairman of the Board, Jim Perkins and the Chairman of the Search Committee,

Daryl Pitts asked if they could come and spend a day with us in Florida.

A week later Vivian awoke and said, "Richard, I had a dream last night that God called us to Friends." I stared at her stunned, "What? Huh."

She shared her dream with me. "There was this beautiful church, full of people. An enthralling choir was singing. Our children were sitting with us on the platform. You were preparing to speak. And then I woke up."

I responded, " That was only a dream." But I knew, all too well, that God sometimes uses dreams to send us messages. After much prayer, we accepted their invitation for a visit.

When they arrived Jim patted my shoulder like I was an old pal of his and said, "We'll be honest with you, we're here to learn all about you, your family, and to answer questions you may have about Friends University."

We spent the entire morning with them touring Gainesville, the university campus, and then hosted them for the afternoon at our home. When we dropped them off at the airport Jim said, "Richard and Vivian, our intent was to sell you on being a serious candidate. You are a wonderful couple and your children are just delightful."

He leaned close as he shook my hand and confided, "You are one of two people the board wanted to vet more freely and we like you."

Daryl said goodbye, "Thanks for letting us take a day out of your busy lives and we hope you will visit us soon." We bid them farewell and told them we would continue to pray about the opportunity and give the decision to God.

We were still not sure we wanted the job. We loved the climate, and the children were making adjustments in their schools. But after much deliberation, we agreed to a visit with the Friend's University board in Wichita.

Vivian and I flew to Kansas not knowing what to expect. We discovered the campus and community were charming. The college was founded in 1889 and gifted from James M. Davis to the Kansas Society of Friends on the condition they start a Quaker college. We ate lunch with the board and had meetings with students and faculty. We learned the university was committed to liberal arts and sciences. They offered a broad-based education for every student, hoping to teach them about personal growth and service from a Christian worldview.

At the end of the day Daryl remarked, "The feedback across campus was very positive today. Have you sensed in any way that you would have further interest in our offer?"

I considered what he shared and replied, "Thank you, Daryl. We have enjoyed our visit, but we would need time to process everything."

We collapsed into our seats on the plane back to Florida. The weight of the decision was hard to carry. Vivian placed her hand in mine and prayed to God for discernment. She then reached over to kiss me and held her face up next to mine." Sweetheart, you were remarkable today in each of your meetings. You listened well and were transparent. You articulated a vision for Christian higher education that was hopeful and attractive. I don't know whether they will call us to make an offer or not, or even if we should take the job, but for the first time I realized you were very presidential. If this isn't God's will, then it will happen somewhere else soon. I love you."

Upon returning to Gainesville, we gathered our three kids together to let them know we were considering the amazing opportunity at Friends. As is often typical, there were three different responses.

Melissa broke down in tears. "Daddy, I don't want to move again. I like my new friends. I like riding my new bicycle with you after school every night." She climbed into her mother's arms and Vivian wiped away her tears. Then Tris interjected, "Gee, I think it will be cool to have my dad be a president." And Doak said matter-of-factly, "Dad, I am not happy with the school I'm in, but I'll be happy with whatever you and mom decide."

The day of reckoning came sooner that we expected. "Dr. Felix, this is Daryl Pitts from Friends University. I have splendid news from our board. This morning they voted unanimously for you to assume the presidency of Friends." I was silent, and he continued. "I'm not sure what you and Vivian have decided, but we hope that you can give us an answer as soon as possible." Part of me was thrilled, and another part took a deep breath in nervous anticipation of this leap of faith.

"Thank you Daryl, we have been in prayer every day about this possibility. Right now I am speechless, except to say we will be back to you right away after I speak to my family." I paused and said, "Thank you for the affirming call."

My family during my time at Bethel and Notre Dame

President of Friends University

7

NEW LEADER IN THE FRIENDS' COMMUNITY

"For this one thing I do, forgetting those things which are behind, and reaching forth unto those things, I press toward the mark for the prize of the high calling of God in Christ Jesus."

~ Philippians 3: 13-14 ~

We accepted the Friends University offer. By the grace of God, I had reached my goal to become the president of a university. Moving from Florida to Kansas was the right decision and allowed our family to settle in one place for a while. Our children settled in at The Wichita Collegiate School, where they found their own community of growth.

On the first day of my presidency, I paused at the bottom of the magnificent stairway leading up to Davis Administration Building. It resembled a Romanesque castle complete with a bell tower, carved statues and exterior buttresses. Was I really in Kansas? Could this be my new office?

Overcome by a strange mixture of awe, elation, and the one hundred degree heat of Wichita, I couldn't breathe. Once inside, my hand was shaking as I opened the door marked the *Office of the President*.

I walked in and noticed a stack of storage containers piled in a corner. I grabbed something out of the box marked Desk Items and sat down at the expansive executive desk. I was holding the box my church had presented to me twenty-two years earlier, the touchstone that had propelled me on my path of Christian higher education.

The box had traveled everywhere with me during the last twenty-two years. It was filled with the keepsakes that had touched and inspired me the most. I shook it a little and lifted the lid.

Memories flooded through my mind as I touched each sacred item: pictures of the green Corvette that was the signature car of my driving school fleet, a photo of my fifth grade class, the joyfully loving faces of my wife and three children, a news clipping of my basketball team at Bethel.

Smiling, I sighed as I pulled out three pennies at the bottom, a token left from the original $34.43 cents my church had donated to my education. Goosebumps ran up my arm and I shook my head as I looked at the well-worn cardboard cigar box which read *Helps in Higher Education*. I closed the box with my heart filled with gratitude and placed it in the top drawer of my desk. The box had come a long way since Lafayette, Indiana. And so had the little abandoned boy.

Soon after my arrival at Friends, I was invited to join the Young Presidents Organization (YPO). It was a group of business leaders that would revolutionize and cultivate my leadership skills and career. Within YPO chapters are forums of ten or fewer leaders from all walks of life who meet for an entire day on a monthly basis to act as an outside board of directors for each other. They give YPO members an opportunity each month to share their critical issues and seek counsel.

At one of my first forum meetings I was asked, "Richard, I don't understand your end goal for this plan. Are you wanting to make your faculty happy or make money for the University?" "Both," I answered.

"Not if I understand your underlying assumptions. There is no way you will make your faculty happy unless you double the size of your budget," he responded. Such would be the back and forth discussions in our meetings, iron sharpening iron. We ask each other tough questions. No skirting the issues. And everything in the forum stays in the forum. No exceptions.

One of those mentors was on my board at Friends. After one board meeting he asked to meet me in my office. "Richard, you blindsided me today with the board. I could have been your ally. Why didn't I know in advance the details about this student issue? I could have helped you if only I had known. Remember Peter Drucker's three rules: Bad news first, no surprises, and finally full disclosure."

For the past thirty years I have been in a similar forum experience with ten wonderful men. Six of us remain today. We have developed a community of openness, trust, and transparency that has dealt with every imaginable life issue both professional and personal - death, divorce, betrayal, business failures as well as many successes. I will almost always point any success to having the wise counsel and advice from these dear life friends.

After being accepted into YPO, I attended a three-day leadership session in Dallas, Texas in which I completed an extensive inventory on leadership skills and attitudes (i.e., Meyers Briggs, Left Brain vs. Right Brain).

They also interviewed me regarding hypothetical situations and challenges I might face. At the end of the analysis, those interviewers explained my leadership strengths, potential weaknesses, and blind spots.

The test used many descriptors for leadership style, such as Wall Street Executive, Religious Leader, Military General, Political leader, Healthcare Executive, Educational leader, Athletic Coach, Media Executive, and Prison Warden. Interestingly, I found out mine was a Conductor.

Peter Drucker often compared successful leaders, especially in universities to symphony conductors: "In some modern symphonies, hundreds of musicians are on stage together and play together. According to organizational theory, there should be several 'group vice-president conductors' and perhaps a dozen 'division conductors.' But there is only one conductor—and every one of the musicians, each a high-grade specialist, plays to that conductor without an intermediary." And so I discovered that my skill set was aligned with my mission. God used this to affirm my calling for what would be a daunting task of rebuilding and revitalizing a small college amidst the backdrop of the economic recession of the early 1980s'.

The eleven years I spent at Friends University flew by. I had wonderful chairmen of the board who nurtured me and provided wisdom for a young president. We were blessed with a generous board of trustees. The cabinet team excelled in each of their areas. Faculties were very student and spiritually oriented and provided outstanding teaching in the classroom while modeling servant leadership.

In the 1980s all of higher education experienced a period of national financial distress and Friends was no exception. Downsizing the college was one of the most difficult assignments of my entire career. The job of cutting budgets and eliminating staff, indeed entire programs, can darken your soul. I needed emotional and spiritual support.

Early one morning I made a call to the Friends' Board Chairman, Jim Perkins. We agreed to have lunch in Howard, Kansas a small agricultural town about seventy miles southeast of Wichita.

Jim was a rancher and oilman. I drove through a rainstorm and finally pulled up to the cafe. I was still in my business suit and tie, including a pair of black wingtip dress shoes. Suddenly my passenger door opened up from the outside. It was Jim. The cowboy hat, rugged looking jacket, and oil field boots literally lifted me out of my Chevrolet as if I was a featherweight. His mammoth arms embraced me as he told me God loved me, and so did he. He placed me back on the dirt road, in a puddle of mud up to my ankles. Goodbye wing tips! I never felt more appreciated and cared for in my life. Wonderful mentors are always there when we need them.

After jumping the hurdle of downsizing, we needed to come up with a strategy to grow the university and increase enrollments again. After considerable research my leadership team launched an adult degree completion program, the first of its kind in the state of Kansas. Soon thereafter we also introduced two master's programs. By 1985, Friends was scaling new heights with record enrollments and new academic programs.

During that period, the physical campus enjoyed a makeover to match its growing student body and academic programs. My team raised substantial capital gifts for new and remodeled facilities. We built a beautiful new student union, the Casado Student Center. We raised money to execute a major overhaul and remodel of the Garvey Athletic Center, which housed our gymnasiums, swimming pool, and athletic training center. Upon completion these sparkling facilities generated enthusiasm, momentum, and an enhanced pride in the campus.

Through these capital campaigns and construction projects, I finally honed my leadership skills to their fullest. I learned to set vision and get buy-in from varied constituencies. I learned how to be transparent in making tough decisions, overcoming bureaucratic resistance and building consensus. A president must always give his campus community hope and a plan for the future.

YPO Forum of Wichita

8

A SURPRISING OFFER

"Be quick but don't hurry."

~ John Wooden ~

n January 1989, my wife Vivian and I had enjoyed a three months sabbatical in Florida. Our goals had been to catch up on much-needed rest and to plan for the next chapter of our eleven years service to Friends' University. But we also knew a difficult, life-changing decision might wait just over the horizon.

The president of Azusa Pacific University had retired, so the university had formed a search committee. Through a nomination by a professional friend, they vetted and identified me as a strong candidate. The committee's chairman, Dr. Ken Ogden, worked to interest Vivian and me in coming on board, calling several times during our sabbatical to engage us in a conversation about taking the job.

Again and again I let him know we were not interested; even if the timing were right, we were not looking to leave Friends University— we had just spent the last three months planning for its future and for our remaining years of work there before retirement. But Dr. Ogden asked us to think about it and said he'd get back in touch after our sabbatical.

True to his word, he called again upon our return to Wichita in April. "Dr. Felix, I appreciate that talking with us is a potential conflict of interest for you. But our search committee is still very interested in having a conversation with you and Vivian."

"And I appreciate your interest," I said, "but Vivian and I have not rented out space in our hearts and minds to explore another presidency."

"I understand. Please, would you and your wife at least make it a matter of prayer?" He was so determined. How could I not agree with this simple, reasonable request?

As Vivian and I discussed the issue, she pressed me about what lessons we had learned during our time of rest and renewal. We had been reading Hannah Whitehall Smith's book, *The Christian's Secret of a Happy Life*, and two things had imprinted us.

First, we should give thanks for everything in our lives, sanctifying it with gratefulness.

Second, we should learn to hold on to things more lightly. Everything we owned and experienced belonged to God, not us; so we needed to be less possessive.

"You have a tendency to refer to Friends as your university," Vivian pointed out. "Perhaps you should reconsider how you think about your role there." That gave me pause. She was probably right. My reticence to even talk with APU betrayed my possessiveness, my tendency to hold onto things too tightly.

I felt personally responsible for assuring that Friends had a promising future. I had made a commitment to the board at my inauguration to steward the college through the uncertain years it had faced. I decided I shouldn't use the word "my" in the future; everything, including Friends University, belonged to God.

Conceding that point to my wife, I thought of another objection. I said that we didn't want to move to Los Angeles, anyway. On my recent fundraising trip to Southern California, I had failed to plan enough time between appointments. Traffic everywhere. The freeways felt put together like tangled spaghetti. Compared to the laid back, wide-open plains of Kansas, there was no contest. I had decided that I would never consider moving my family to Los Angeles. Vivian couldn't disagree that the cost of moving to a crowded, high-stress environment would be high.

One day, I made a list of the pros and cons to at least begin a conversation with APU. I sat down at my computer and started typing. When I finished, I hit the print button, grabbed the sheet from the printer, and lay down on the bed to review and peruse the information. No sooner had I reclined against my pillows than the phone rang. Vivian picked it up and after a second announced, "It's Dr. Ken Ogden calling again from California."

"Dr. Felix, I just wanted to circle back and see if you and Vivian had time to reconsider and pray about APU. I also want to give you some reasons you might find APU attractive." As he named them one by one, I realized they were almost identical to the ones on my list before me! I shook my head, thinking, How like God to work this way!

After assuring Dr. Ogden that I'd get back to him soon, I told Vivian everything he had said, and I showed her my list. Perhaps God was up to something here. The offer filled our minds with questions. Why were we down there in Florida for those three months getting much needed rest and renewal for our hearts and souls? Could it be that we needed that time away from Friends to open us to other possibilities God might have for us? We had always believed that sensing God's calling was essential to make important life decisions. Was this one of those divine moments?

As soon as I had finished my call with Dr. Ogden, I researched online about the history of APU. They founded the University in 1899 as the Training School of Christian Workers in Whittier. Two women, Mary Hill and Mary Draper, wanted to train young men and women to respond to the social needs of that time in Los Angeles. They both had Quaker backgrounds. One of their mission outreaches each year was to Central America, in which both teachers and students ministered together. Many missionaries contracted diseases during trips to various countries. Some of them died because of their infections. I discovered that the spirit of service at APU was still pervasive over 100 years later.

The school had several name changes over the years. After many years of various presidents a youthful man, Cornelius Haggard, would take the presidency and hold it for thirty-six years. He led the school to its relocation to Azusa, and it grew and benefited from mergers from both LA Pacific College in 1965 and Arlington College in 1968.

The University would receive WASC accreditation and add master's degrees. Its present enrollment when we assumed the presidency in 1989 was around 2100 students and operated with a budget of $22 million.

My serving at a Quaker college in Wichita provided a connection to APU theologically. The university's theological persuasion and practice was ultimately Wesleyan Arminian, which was my upbringing as a child and adult. Both were attributes that piqued my interest.

"What if God truly is calling us to leave Wichita for Southern California?" Vivian said. "What harm would it be to at least listen to Dr. Ogden?" So, for the next several days we prayed together and asked God for guidance and clearness to pursue the APU opportunity.

One morning soon thereafter, I said that I thought God was using Dr. Ogden's persistence to get our attention. Vivian agreed, "You always talk about having options, and maybe this is one we need to explore. Why don't you give Dr. Ogden a call today?"

With her encouragement and a sense of peace, I did just that. It pleased him to receive my call, and I consented to his request to forward a copy of my vitae and résumé for his committee.

The APU recruitment team aggressively courted us despite our lingering apprehension about completing our work at Friends University. A whirlwind of activities and wooing with APU followed for the next six weeks. Dr. Ogden and two other members of his search committee, Don Marshburn and Jack Rankin, wished to come to campus during the upcoming Friends' Alumni weekend in mid-April. They wanted to have private meetings with us off-campus and to see me in action, giving speeches, making awards, providing introductions—just being presidential.

The APU trio arrived on a Thursday and we entertained them for dinner at our home near campus. From the very beginning they put us at ease as they told us about their families, their own careers, and Azusa Pacific.

The next two days we had time for discussions at our home and a tour of the campus, having casual conversations with students, faculty, and alums. Throughout the weekend's festivities, they pretended to be alumni - sitting through the dinner at which I spoke, standing in the back of the auditorium while I presented the Outstanding Alumni awards, and even attending the Singing Quakers concert. It was amusing to listen to the three men dodge questions about who they were, what they were doing on campus, and what year they had graduated. Vivian, our son Doak, and I enjoyed a Sunday brunch with them.

Little did I know that the seeds of a lifetime friendship with these three gentlemen were being planted. They would become my partners in leading the APU board through its transformation over the next decade.

Ken Ogden, Don Marshburn, and Jack Rankin were not only first-class Christian gentlemen but also they were also leaders in their various professions. Ken led the Counseling Program for Focus on the Family, Don was CEO of a successful seed company in Southern California, and Jack was Superintendent of a large Los Angeles area school district serving over 45,000 students. Don and Jack would serve with distinction as Chairmen of the Board at APU, providing valuable counsel and insight to my leadership. Both of them and other members of my board would become valuable mentors who spoke into my life regularly.

A few days later, after the Alumni Weekend, Dr. Ogden called again. "Dr. Felix, I have one last request. Would you be open to one other board member from APU spending a day with you next week?" I replied, "Certainly."

"Great. Our board member, Dr. Ted Engstrom, will call you to arrange the visit." My mind and heart started racing. *The* Ted Engstrom from World Vision fame was coming to visit me? I had read several of his books and quoted him frequently in my speeches and board reports. He was already a significant influence in my life. Part of me was shaking in my boots, but his phone call the next day put me at ease. He said he had contacted a few of his friends in Christian higher education and he looked forward to our time together.

The following week, I drove to the Wichita Airport to meet Dr. Ted. He carried a large briefcase in one hand and a Wall Street Journal in the other, a giant of a man. During the interview he peppered me with questions about life at Friends University, the choices I had made and the processes behind those decisions. I asked him several questions as well about APU.

He noted I appeared to be a driven person with a penchant for excellence saying I reminded him of his younger days. Leaning forward, he spoke intently, "Where does all of this passion for excellence come from? Do you sense that God has a deeper calling for your life? If so, what does that look like? And could that personal vision be a part of APU's future?"

His query made me pause for a moment to reach my collected thoughts deep inside. Then I unpacked a dream I had for Christian higher education based on the colorful mix of my formal education and varied experience. I explained to Dr. Ted that during the past eleven years at Friends' University; I had plenty of time to conceptualize what my future vision and calling might look like. It was a dream that became my passion.

I paused and said, "Before answering your question, I would ask you to set the stage to hear my answer with grace and humility. I believe that a powerful desire to do something is a gift from God. And when He gives us a thirst for excellence, He always provides the means, the people, the finances, and an appropriate time and a place to achieve it. So here's my dream." He smiled and considered my words.

"I would love to see an interdenominational Evangelical university in America that would someday be what Notre Dame is to Catholics, Brandeis is to the Jewish community and Baylor is to the Baptists. The foundation of this institution would be Christ-honoring excellence. The size of total enrollments, both undergraduate and graduate would not be greater than 10,000 students. Top scholars from around the world would be attracted to the campus because of the quality and scope of the research environment."

He sat up in his chair as I continued, "The school would have a diverse undergraduate population that would not exceed eight-thousand students so we could still retain the sense of community in chapel and other common experiences. All members of the university would have love and gratitude for each other."

"The doctoral programs, with their particular Christian worldview, would prepare future leaders for the nearly one-hundred and sixty colleges of the CCCU and for all the arenas of professional life."

I took a deep breath and continued, "Students and faculty would be involved in outreach programs throughout the world, not just in their local setting. Those outside of the university would sense a community driven by a passion to serve others. National media would reach out first to staff and scholars on this campus for answers to the pertinent issues of the day.

I told Dr. Ted that if God called me to APU, I would love to begin the work of establishing a flagship for excellence in higher education. Such a task would be a twenty to fifty-year journey of committed leadership by the university's board, but I would relish the challenge to begin such a grand vision.

Dr. Ted then asked, "Richard, can that vision be achieved here in Wichita?"

I hesitated, "Unfortunately, probably not. This dream mostly likely would only be accomplished in a larger metropolitan area where resources were much more plentiful to attract and hire great faculty, establish partnerships, and secure the vast amounts of capital needed to fund such an undertaking."

He reached his hand across the table and said, "Richard, you are coming to Southern California to be the President at

APU." I responded, "But Dr. Engstrom, you are not on the search committee."

"Who do you think sent me here today?" He laughed. "They will finalize the offer with my recommendation."

After dropping Dr. Ted off at the Wichita Airport, Vivian and I sat down for dinner. She asked how our visit had gone. I responded, "I think we had better prepare ourselves for living in California."

She was not surprised by what I said. "He offered you the job?" I shrugged my shoulders and smiled with a quizzical grin, "I think so."

There are often those special times when God seems to open a door to an opportunity after we have invested ourselves in a dream, but this job offer was bigger than we could imagine.

It sure seemed like this was one of those once in a lifetime opportunities. And how could I say no if God's messenger was Dr. Ted, and he was resonating with my dream? This was the key to making our decision to move to California if the job offer came. I could look forward to being mentored by him and fulfilling my dreams.

A day later I received a follow-up phone call from Ken Ogden, who said the APU board was excited to meet with us. Somehow we found a three-day window in our schedule to visit the APU campus. Before leaving for California, we prayed for discernment. Did APU share our point of view for excellence, and Dr. Engstrom's support for our vision? Would the campus community be ready for the challenge of creating a premiere Christian University?

Search Committee: Jack Rankin, Ted Engstrom, Don Marshburn

9

FAITH IN GOD'S MISSION

"Life is either a daring adventure or nothing at all."

~ Helen Keller ~

We arrived on the APU campus for the very first time while Chapel was underway, the atmosphere electric. When we walked in, there wasn't a seat to be found anywhere; students were standing against the walls and so were we. The spine-rippling music and a few of them who were dancing in the aisles captivated us. The spirit of joy and community seemed like a light warm rain from Heaven.

Dr. Ron Cline was the speaker that day, and he challenged the congregation to step out of their comfort zones to serve God. The students' verbal and nonverbal responses were spontaneous and heartfelt. Vivian and I stood with tears in our eyes and held each other's hands, basking in the presence of the Holy Spirit, who seemed to be wooing us to APU through the students' display of spiritual vibrancy.

Until now, we had seen our vision through our minds' eyes. Now we were seeing our calling through our hearts. This may have been the actual moment we knew we were called to APU.

Still glowing from the Chapel experience, we joined the Board of Trustees for lunch. We sat at the side of the room, and I was introduced then invited to the table. I told them that Vivian and I were a team and I wished her to join me. We spent the afternoon in dialogue with them. We had a list of questions for them and they had plenty of thoughtful queries of their own, mostly about our family and personal life.

Our three-day visit sped by, and we were soon on our way back to the airport. Someone on campus had given us a copy of the LA Times to read and suggested we peruse the Sports section for a story about the APU track and field coach, Dr. Terry Franson.

The sportswriter noted APU's many consecutive NAIA national championships and mentioned how that year's team was once again on the precipice of winning another championship. But two APU All-American athletes had broken the honor code, changing everything. Dr. Franson suspended them from participating in the national tournaments, costing APU the championship by just a few points. The sportswriter unpacked the story, noting that at many major universities this infraction would have never resulted in more than a verbal slap on the wrist.

We were impressed by Coach Franson's integrity. There was no bending or ignoring the rules; they applied to everyone, including star athletes. A solid example that having God First on the APU logo was not just another slogan, but being lived out by one of its coaches.

A week later, a box arrived from APU's Dean of Students, Jon Wallace, filled with hundreds of cards from students. He had asked the students in the chapel to write on a card describing what they desired in a new president and spouse. We opened the box just before retiring for the evening and laughed and cried as we read each card. This touched us. Again we felt called and reaffirmed with our decision. We could imagine sharing our lives with these students.

We also sought wisdom from our inner circle, which included most notably our family and our YPO group. Our wonderful children were college students themselves—Tris and Melissa attended college in North Carolina while Doak stayed and did his post baccalaureate work at the University of Kansas—and our potential move would not directly affect their lives. Their message to us was, "Follow your hearts." One of them said lightheartedly, "Remember Dad, you might be the University president but Mom is the CEO of Intuition. Listen to her."

Our Young Presidents forum of eight Kansas business leaders wanted to know whether I sensed both a deep calling and an interesting reason to bring forth my vision into California, and throughout our conversation, they worked hard at sifting that out.

One of these men said to me, "I remember you inherited a tough financial situation when you first arrived at Friends a decade ago. We watched you overcome each challenge you faced, and it strengthened you and made you wiser. You know what the future looks like here and you have spent a sabbatical preparing for the next leg of the journey. And you do not understand what you will face in California. I think the best times are just ahead. Why not stay and enjoy the fruits of your labor?"

Another offered a different view, "If you feel satisfied with your work at Friends, then perhaps it's a good time to hand the baton off to a new leader who may have a different skill set that Friends' needs to move into the future."

As we talked, this line of thinking became stronger and stronger. One thing they said still rings clear in my mind:

"Richard, you are a builder. An entrepreneur. A change agent, not a caretaker. You've been able to create wonderful programs at Friends, and you've returned from your sabbatical with plans to maintain what you've built. But builders are often not good maintainers. So, wouldn't the APU opportunity be a better fit for where you are in your life right now?"

What a blessing to have so many colleagues and friends to call on when making a major life changing decision. I have always believed leaders who have valuable mentors in their lives often make the best future trailblazers. At least in my career that was the case.

And now we were awaiting word from the APU search committee and the board's decision. Vivian and I knew that we would hear from them within days and we also felt that our time in Wichita was probably short.

So, on a lovely Kansas evening with a gorgeous sunset waning in the distance, we took a stroll around the beautiful Friends campus that was bursting with spring colors. Our maintenance crew did a marvelous job keeping the grounds looking like a million dollars.

A choir was singing in the Riney Hall of Music, their voices flowing through openings into the outside world. The library and the new Casado Student Center were a hubbub of students studying for final exams. The windows of the buildings reflected the darkening shades of blue from the sky.

We stopped and prayed on the top steps of historic Davis Hall. These were the very steps where we had given our inaugural address nearly eleven years earlier. We gazed out the circle drive toward our home on University Avenue and Vivian said, "You've been silent. What are you thinking?" I couldn't answer, too overtaken by the weight of our history there and how it was probably coming to an end. We walked to the bottom of the long entry steps to Davis and looked back up to the Bell Tower.

Never one to give up, Vivian asked again what I was pondering. "I'm recalling our time in Florida a few months ago," I finally said. "I'm thanking God for this incredible tenure we've enjoyed. I am trying to tenderly hold the faculty, board members, donors, thousands of students and the hundreds of friendships we nurtured all over Wichita. We invested so much of our lives here at Friends. Just walking around campus tonight makes leaving painful to think about."

"But what does that mean for us?" I said, "Honey, I think you know what it means. Everything seems to nudge us toward California. It's hard to ignore. If we get the offer at APU, we have to think about it seriously."

Vivian placed her hand around my neck and said, "We've given Friends our best. The school is in good shape and has a promising future. What we saw and heard around campus this evening will be in our memories forever. No one will ever be able to take them away from us. Perhaps we have fulfilled our calling to Friends." I nodded. I was so blessed to have Vivian as my soul mate and life partner. Together we were feeling released from Friends.

We walked around the Circle Drive and back down the street to the President's home, tears streaming down our cheeks. Saying goodbye would not be easy.

Sure enough, within the week we received the call from Dr. Ogden. He said that the Board had just made a unanimous decision to offer us the presidency of Azusa Pacific. Had we also decided?

By this time, Vivian and I knew we felt called, and we acknowledged this to Dr. Ogden. He said he would happily relay our answer to the board.

Two special memories especially blessed our family during our time at Friends. The first occurred a few years earlier at our Friends Commencement when I presented my son, Doak, his undergraduate degree. As he crossed the platform, he wrapped me in his loving arms as I handed him his diploma. This is the same baby boy I held twenty-one years earlier.

Doak's graduation announcement was added to my sacrosanct memory box as I took it out of my desk and packed up my Friend's University office belongings to once again take a leap of faith and begin a new life in California.

Our second highlight was bringing Shelly Cui from China to live with us. Shelly's grandfather and Vivian's father were brothers. She first earned a degree at Friends University and ultimately an MBA at APU. Our family adopted her as our own. Shelly's father ZC would become a guest professor on our campus.

Historic Painting of Davis Hall

We flew to APU for their commencement, to sign a contract and spend time with the board once again. We settled on August 1, 1990 as our first day on the job and scheduled a Board retreat soon thereafter in Orange County to get to know each other and start planning. It would be an important occasion to listen to the board and share the initial components of our vision for a God-first flagship university.

PART THREE
COMMITMENT TO SCHOLARSHIP

10

EMBRACING THE APU PRESIDENCY

"When you give someone your time, you are giving them a portion of your life that you will never get back. Your time is your life. That is why the greatest gift you can give someone is your time."

~ Rick Warren ~

I was eager to begin my work at APU. My vision of what could be would become my destiny. I wanted to assemble an orchestra of faculty with the music that beckoned me. "Remember," Vivian smiled, "You are the conductor, not the owner."

There were many advantages to just having completed an eleven-year presidency at another institution. I knew from experience that I would have only one opportunity to gain genuine input from all the stakeholders at APU. I was eager to listen and learn their perspectives and opinions and their dreams and hopes for the future. There is a familiar saying; *People don't care about what you know unless they believe that you care.*

With this goal in mind, I traveled several times from Kansas to APU over this summer to meet with all stakeholder groups. I started with the faculty and staff whom I met in small groups of twelve for about an hour each. I asked each person to tell me about their position on campus, positive directions in place, possibilities for change or improvement, and what they expected from me as president. As the "listener-in-chief", I had to place my fingers on the pulse of the campus so I could ease any uncertainty during the presidential transition. Our open communication was essential.

During one of these meetings, a faculty member at the end of the table leaned forward with a raised hand and said, "My major expectation is for you to be the person I can trust." All eyes turned back toward me and several nodded in agreement. It was a powerful moment because it made me realize that if trust did not exist, our dreams would crumble before we could even lay the first brick. I became determined to deliver a culture that would be open, transparent, inclusive, and celebratory. As major players in the symphony yet to be written, they were most deserving of this respect.

Shortly after this meeting, several of the faculty members encouraged me to hike the Garcia Trail with them. The trail stood right above the campus in the San Gabriel Mountains and offered a grand view of the APU campus and beyond. I jumped all in.

The two-mile trek up and back was challenging, but the view at the top was breathtaking. As I stood on the crest of the mountain, I could see the sun reflecting against the backdrop of Orange County overlooking the Pacific Ocean that stretched far to the horizon, west where the City of Angels skyline poked out of the haze to the north of Los Angeles. The mountains of the San Fernando Valley ran like a wall between the city and the desert. I prayed that our call to APU might some day have an impact for Jesus Christ much as Mary Hill had envisioned her labors a century before.

During administrative meetings that summer, I soon discovered that the Cabinet was a major strength for the University and I felt fortunate to have inherited such a highly gifted team to be the lead musicians. Don Grant, Cliff Hamlow, Hank Bode, and David Lambert were seasoned veterans. All these men were critical to building a future of excellence, sharing the same vision, and developing strategies to bring that vision to reality.

I have always believed the gifts of a team might never match, but their limitations must never match. If collective weaknesses exist, the result is blind spots that lead to poor decisions. During summer conversations with this team of vice presidents, it seemed clear they were qualified and a sense of common trust had developed between us. I was confident that all of them could play a solo whenever the occasion demanded.

Students are always at the heart of a university - the core of my dream and the point of my vision. So getting to know the student leaders was a top priority. That summer I cast aside my business attire for jeans and hiking shoes to take part with them at both the Walkabout in the High Sierras and the Bridges Program in the Tenderloin district of San Francisco. Hiking in the Sierras, sitting around the campfire at night listening to their hearts, and serving meals in the run-down hotels of the Tenderloin for those dying of

AIDS deepened my desire to serve the university and these young people. They were the genuine face, energy, and voice of APU.

Later that month, on the last Saturday of summer before school started, we had another most memorable experience with these students. We had just moved into the President's Home and that night collapsed into bed feeling an odd combination of exhaustion and boundless energy. The muffled sounds of laughter and talking entered my dreams throughout the night. In the morning something tugged me out of bed—the smells of savory bacon and sweet cinnamon rolls. Stumbling to peek out the window, I saw sleeping bags strewn on the front lawn, each with someone's body inside. One student stood nearby wearing an APU sweatshirt and eating a strawberry from our garden. Laden with coffee and donuts from the Donut Man and bubbling with enthusiasm, the students had come to welcome us to APU. We discovered their sincerity when we found Felix the Cat seat covers on our car later that day.

Close to summer's end, the Board of Trustees weekend retreat was celebrated at an off-campus location in Orange County. I had already met many of the board members during the selection process, but now I had the opportunity to learn more about them and to discuss the work of the board. Just like composers, our job was to discuss dreams and concerns for the university while holding the essence of the score in their hands: God-First.

At the onset of our meeting, I presented changes regarding the board's work including: a broadening of committee focus on substantive issues; the creation of a committee on trusteeship; term limits on board service; inclusion of staff, faculty, students to be present at board meetings; and an annual evaluation of the university president. When I finished detailing these proposals, a few of the Board of Trustees sat in silence. This was unfamiliar territory for some. There was some resistance within the board and it seemed like an uphill battle we all had to climb together. Fortunately, the Executive Committee and Chairman Don Marshburn were supportive and in the months ahead we adopted the recommendations. Mozart may have written a major symphony in a couple of days, but most innovators need the gift of time to create a masterpiece.

It satisfied me we had planted the seeds for culture change within the top levels of the university, beginning to make our campus a more open, healthy community. Having the board's full support would be necessary for all future work toward developing a flagship university.

Marilyn Schulz, Administrative Assistant, my first and best hire!

Freshman Mugging Party

View from the top of the Garcia Trail

11

IMAGINATION IN POSSIBILITIES

"When people with talent work together, expect a miracle."

~ Lee Iacocca ~

In the early Fall of 1990 after a few months on campus, I scheduled an audience with Dr. Ernie Boyer, President of the Carnegie Foundation for the Advancement of Teaching. Dr. Boyer had authored several reports for the Carnegie Foundation, which had a significant impact on the nation's educational agenda for several decades. Actually, he had been walking by my side for years on my leadership journey. Now I was meeting him face to face.

"Good morning, Dr. Felix, welcome to Princeton and the Carnegie Foundation. I have been looking forward to meeting you. My brother Bill, your Dean of Arts and Sciences is delighted that we were having this time to meet each other."

"Thanks, Dr. Boyer, I am grateful for this opportunity to meet you and review the in-depth study you and your colleagues conducted for APU in 1988, *A Community of Teaching and Learning: Striking the Balance.*"

Dr. Boyer and his visiting team had spent a considerable amount of time on campus researching the academic climate and interviewing students, faculty, staff, administration, and board of trustee members. His report to the Azusa Pacific community offered a list of recommendations he felt was crucial to the APU's continuing progress. The Carnegie Report's primary recommendations were:

1. APU's important commitment to a 'community of caring' should be balanced with a continued commitment to build a solid academic foundation.
2. The administrative leadership should be balanced by expanded faculty development and involvement in the institution's governance.

My primary interest was his response to another statement in the report: Azusa Pacific has made dramatic progress and is ready to move up to a whole additional level of significance—as a community and as an educational institution." What did he mean by that?

Dr. Boyer paused for a moment and said, "APU's culture of spiritual vibrancy is its major asset. I sensed a strong ethos of a caring community and your faculty delivers knowledge and commitment to their students. This unique combination of spirituality and scholarship provides a firm foundation for APU's growth."

Dr. Boyer turned the question back to me, "President Felix, what attracted you to APU and what are some of your dreams and your overall vision?" I unpacked my vision to establish an interdenominational university that would be a flagship for Christian higher education and beyond.

I shared my plans for ultimately making APU a national university replete with doctoral programs attracting the finest scholars. In my mind, without a top rate faculty, becoming a flagship would only be a pipe dream.

But the first step toward that grand goal was to elevate the role of faculty in institutional governance. I shared the findings of my summer visits to campus, in which faculty felt that they were not involved in decisions that could strengthen the university. I told him I had already addressed this issue at the August board retreat and they received it well, but there was not yet unanimous support for my proposal to have faculty and students represented at all board meetings.

I believed reducing faculty loads and increasing faculty salaries were also top priorities in attracting a faculty of excellence. The Southern California "adult degree completion" market was as yet untapped for Christian colleges and we intended to engage this population base with quality programs fitting APU's mission and purpose. The financial margins from these programs would enable APU to reduce faculty workloads and raise salaries at the same time. Our goal was to have APU faculty salaries second only to Wheaton among CCCU institutions within five years.

Both goals would enable APU to recruit a higher quality and diverse faculty, which would bring the ultimate doctoral program goals into a clearer, more obtainable reality. A high-quality faculty with substantial input to govern the University would allow APU to achieve a vision Dr. Boyer had outlined in his Carnegie Report: "We believe Azusa Pacific is becoming a leader among colleges and universities willing to combine an unapologetic commitment to Christianity with an uncompromising commitment to educational excellence."

Dr. Boyer responded to my vision thoughtfully, tempered with astute observations. He suggested that being in Los Angeles, a major city of world influence and diversity, would be huge for not only attracting financial support but for recruiting quality faculty. Likewise, the Los Angeles basin would offer a sizable population of adult students for undergraduate and master's degree completion and for my proposed doctoral programs. He jokingly added that the warmer climate wouldn't hurt either.

He thought APU's interdenominational posture was a major calling card for becoming a flagship university. He thought smaller denominational schools would always have difficulty making a more national case for existence.

Finally, Dr. Boyer hypothesized that the diversity of population in Southern California would strengthen APU's mission to become a flagship university as it entered the next century.

He wrote in the Carnegie Report, "There are few colleges and universities today that can combine a rich sense of academic rigor with an equally vigorous commitment to moral education. Azusa Pacific University has the potential for being one of those rare and cherished institutions."

Then he said, "Your present campus is probably too small. Further, it is landlocked and the board would probably need to find another location in which to expand the school at some future date to accomplish your vision of a flagship campus."

He reminded me that the present APU campus resulted from several relocations and merging of other colleges; making another move to a new location shouldn't be that difficult. He thought APU had not established a geographical footprint that couldn't be abandoned at this point in its history. He noted that he liked APU's present location because it was embedded within the larger LA basin, enabling it to fulfill its 100-year-old original mission: that APU serve as a witness and light for Christ in the city of Angels.

This had been a formative visit for me as APU's new president. It honored me that a man of his distinction and character would spend such quality time with me.

He resonated with several of my ideas to ratchet up the academic culture, to further ingrain spiritual vibrancy among students and faculty, and to move toward doctoral program development. He warned me that others in the academy and accreditation community might offer considerable resistance, i.e., your own faculty, other college presidents, WASC accreditation.

Dr. Boyer's words resounded in my mind long after I returned from Princeton. I connected his support of my vision as a matching bookend with that of Dr. Engstrom's several months earlier in Wichita.

I had already begun building trust and a culture of excellence by sowing the seeds of change in governance, but as Dr. Boyer predicted, space was a colossal problem—both in land and several buildings. If we could build doctoral programs and attract world-class faculty, how could we find the resources for such a monumental task?

Every question has an answer and one just germinated in my builder's mind. The answer to the question asked at Princeton came sooner than expected. It was practically standing at my front door when I got back to California. It was Mrs. Naomi Wilden, a petite, lovely woman with a heart of gold and a passion for APU. She and her late husband had been donors to the university for years. We had invited her to visit campus with Vivian and me. A delightful woman, she talked glowingly about our students during lunch.

"Oh, I just love coming to campus and mingling with your students. They have so much passion and energy. There is such a sense of spiritual vibrancy that radiates through them. I especially love hearing from the choir at Christmas time. I have so many of their CDs in my library."

I expressed our gratitude for her generosity over the years and asked more about her interest in the university and how their involvement began.

"My late husband, Jim, and I have received immense pleasure investing in the school financially. Are you planning any new projects or buildings?" she implored. Her query stopped us short and brought smiles to our faces. I mentioned two or three building projects to solve basic space issues on campus, but she showed little interest in any of them. In a moment of uncomfortable silence, Vivian was giving me a funny look. I was drowning and needed a lifeline. Finally, Vivian came to the rescue.

"Richard, why don't you tell Mrs. Wilden about the beautiful business building you've been dreaming to build one day." That suggestion was the game changer.

Mrs. Wilden's countenance changed immediately. "Jim invented and designed the Double Diaphragm Pump and eventually established the Wilden Pump Company." We listened to her story and then I painted a picture of the building, its features and purpose. I suggested that perhaps the primary conference room could be a museum for the Double Diaphragm Pump.

"Tell me more, Dr. Felix. How much would it cost? What size of gift would it take to name it?" I took a deep breath and replied, "We do not have an exact number but our best estimate is around five million dollars. To name a building we would need 50% of the cost to build."

She smiled again and said, "That is a project that would bring me great joy. It would be a testament to my husband's hard work and devotion to making a difference. I would like to fund this from our foundation."

Dr. Ernie Boyer, President of Carnegie Foundation

Groundbreaking of Business Building with Naomi Wilden

Wilden Hall of Business

12

APU INAUGURATION

"The best way to predict the future is to create it."

~ Peter Drucker ~

One of the most memorable and pleasurable days of my life was January 29, 1991. On the day of my inauguration, it was a beautiful, warm California day in the APU Football Stadium with the stunning San Gabriel Mountains as a backdrop.

My beloved wife Vivian and our children Doak, Tristram, and Melissa were by my side on the platform. Family and friends had joined us from around the nation. Delegates and friends from colleges and universities far and near joined our board, faculty, and staff in a rainbow of academic colors. City and state leaders dotted the well-wishers, and even the respected Dr. Ernest Boyer attended. I felt humbled yet challenged by their presence.

After the preliminary tributes, congratulations, and challenging remarks from the dignitaries on the platform, I strode to the podium to unpack my vision for Azusa Pacific University.

"For APU to achieve its potential and live up to its promise, that higher vision, which I will paint with a broad brush, must be based on these commitments: first, Christ; second, diversity; third, service; and fourth, community. Without any hesitation, I pledge to you that quality will be the hallmark of all we do."

I posited two primary reasons APU ought to become a leader in higher education and a flagship for Christian colleges and universities. First, APU's distinctive character and spirit flowed from her critical strength of mission and purpose. The 1988 US News and World Report, which ranked APU in the top 25 smaller comprehensive universities in America, evidenced this.

Second, APU's strategic location in Southern California was an untapped strength. Southern California was no longer just the western edge of our nation, but the unofficial capital of the Pacific Rim cultures with proximity to two-thirds of the world's population.

I reminded the audience that the Carnegie Foundation for the Advancement of Education had this to say about APU's potential: "We are confident that APU can go beyond conventional procedures and make the institution a model for the nation, blending, in creative ways, the curricular and co-curricular life on campus."

Many inaugural addresses deal in generalities about an institution's values and promise to keep those traditions alive. Specific goals and promises are not always included within those remarks. But, I wanted my inaugural address to have a heavy emphasis on specific programs and projects, so I talked about the following goals clearly and succinctly:

1. Involving faculty, staff, and students in board strategic planning and governance.
2. Increasing faculty salaries while decreasing faculty load.
3. Increasing the number of faculty with terminal degrees.
4. An openness and commitment to innovation & creativity, designing then crafting APU's future.
5. Recruiting a more diverse faculty, staff, and student body.
6. Developing a degree completion program for adult learners.
7. Developing a rich array of service opportunities for students and faculty.
8. Expanding our physical location for needed faculty space and student housing.
9. Becoming a doctoral granting institution.

I closed my address with this bold and optimistic forecast, "At Azusa Pacific's centennial celebration in 1999, I see a university modeling the way for our nation. Quality, Diversity, Community, and Service will pervade campus life. Five to seven new buildings will complement those on campus today."

"Selected doctoral programs flowing out of strong undergraduate and master's programs will provide diverse opportunities for students from around the world. Students of all ages from diverse cultural backgrounds will integrate God's great love on this campus, and their natural response will be to go into all parts of the world to share that love with others."

I ended my remarks by announcing the seven-figure gift from Mrs. Naomi Wilden to help fund a new business building to be named, *The Wilden Hall of Business*. And then I shared the good news about construction of a new residence hall.

As important as the speech was for unpacking and outlining a vision for the future of APU, I knew that revealing the Wilden gift and the board's decision to erect a new residence hall would provide tangible evidence that change was already well on its way—that with God's blessing and leading we would become a flagship university.

These buildings were the first down payment on our inaugural promises, showing that I would be a promise keeper. Nothing builds trust within your community like keeping your promises. They would also help build early momentum, which I have learned from experience is not an easy feat.

I also wanted the inauguration to be a time to celebrate nine decades of keeping *God First*, a time to celebrate God's goodness and faithfulness. My invaluable friend Dr. Jack Rankin chaired the entire inaugural event, and it was a day to celebrate God's goodness at APU.

The welcoming line following the ceremony seemed to last forever. So many friends and well-wishers to meet and greet. They overwhelmed Vivian and me with their responses.

A couple of fellow presidential colleagues particularly amused me from very prominent, private, and elitist Southland colleges. After congratulating me on a well-presented address, they subtly reminded me that APU's mission was to train teachers, missionaries, and other helping professions. They didn't believe we could provide doctoral programs. I smiled and thanked them for their opinions. I said I looked forward to working in cooperation with them as our level of scholarship increased among our faculty.

In the line was a long-time faculty member who said to me, "Wonderful speech, Dr. Felix. But I want you to know that they hired me to teach here when the school was a Bible College. Later I had to adjust to the school becoming a Christian liberal arts college. Another incoming president added master's programs and changed us to a university. And now you are calling for us to become a national university of excellence with doctoral programs. I am not sure I am ready for this."

I said, "Hasn't God always been faithful through each of these changes?" He nodded in the affirmative and I asked, "Has our commitment to *God First* been kept at each period of change?"

Again he smiled and confessed that it had indeed remained at the core of APU's life. I said, "Then let's make the Mary Hills and Cornelius Haggards proud by completing the dreams they had for that little Bible College!"

That evening, following a lengthy series of events including the symposium featuring Dr. Ernest Boyer and a concert by University Choir, Vivian and I slipped into our car to drive home.

She leaned over and said, "Honey, you were great today. You always amaze me with your excitement, with ideas and the energy to project vision. But even if you can raise millions of dollars to build a bunch of new buildings, where are you going to put them on our little postage stamp campus? Those are huge promises you have made." They were indeed. But I had confidence that they were God inspired.

APU **Life**

AzusaPacificUniversity

Summer 1990

Introducing
Dr. Richard E. Felix
Azusa Pacific University's
15th President

Inside: Spotlight on Leadership
Individuals who
"set the pace" at APU

Cover of APU Life Magazine

Dr. Jack Rankin, Chair of the Inauguration

13

BUILDING THE FUTURE

"Success comes in a lot of ways, but it doesn't come with money and it doesn't come with fame. It comes with having a life of meaning."

~ Tim Tebow ~

ess than a month after my inauguration, Dr. Hank Bode, one of our Vice Presidents hurried into my office one day with extraordinary news. The Avery Dennison (AD) corporate property located two blocks from our campus had been placed on the market for sale.

We drove to the property and explored the twenty acres, complete with a beautiful executive office building fronting Foothill Boulevard and three tilt-up warehouse/storage facilities at the back of the property. It could provide an additional 250,000 square feet of space for us.

That very next day we gathered several cabinet members and deans together in the middle of the AD parking lot for a prayer session. "Dear Lord, is there any way you could use this property for your glory through APU? If so, go before us and open the doors for its purchase."

Soon other APU board members gathered to tour the facilities and quickly approved our investigation into purchasing the property. APU was blessed to have the talents and gifts of one of our board members, Mr. Winston Ko, to serve as the point person to negotiate with Avery Dennison. As an architect and businessman, Winston's knowledge, wisdom, and creativity led to the successful acquisition of the property.

Through a creative arrangement, Avery-Dennison could benefit tax-wise while selling for a significantly reduced price to APU—a charitable 403(c) not-for-profit institution. The kicker in the deal was that AD leased back the tilt-up buildings from APU for the next three years, thus lowering the actual price the University paid for the property and buildings by three million. It was a win-win for both parties.

The acquisition of this new property was a catalyst for an incredible growth spurt. In the next several years we would add two adjoining properties bringing the total west campus footprint to over fifty acres, thus equaling the size of the original east campus.

Thanks to this miracle gift from God, our inauguration plan to build several buildings was taking shape. Overnight it would provide the space to accommodate our impending explosion in enrollment growth. The blank canvas for our dreams just got bigger.

About this same time, I received a friendly letter in the mail from Mr. Richard Stack from the Darling Foundation with a check expressing appreciation for an APU student who had been a babysitter for his children. The quality of this young woman who extremely impressed him triggered his interest in learning more about APU. I invited him to campus for chapel and lunch, and he loved meeting students so much that he asked us to send him a proposal for a campus need, which I did. Thus began a wonderful relationship with the Darling Foundation.

In due time, Mr. Stack informed us of the Foundation's desire to make the major lead gift towards a new library on the West Campus. It would be our first signature building for that part of the university—a twenty-first century state-of-the-art library. Again, this generous gift propelled us forward to our goal.

As the semester quickly gathered steam, we created a campus-wide study group to build a culture of inclusion and trust through the creation of the Four Cornerstones of APU. After several meetings encompassing three months this faculty-driven study group collaborated and completed its work, naming Christ the chief cornerstone along with Scholarship, Community, and Service. These four cornerstones were to be the focal point for everything we did on campus in the present and into the future.

The last task of the group was to develop a university brand that captured the essence of these cornerstones. Branding is the first line of communication to everyone inside the community and to the outside world, so we had to get it right. We worked with a professional outside agency to develop the right brand strategy, including the logo that still appears today on all university materials.

At the center of the logo is the cross. Surrounding the cross on four sides are stones representing the four cornerstones. The largest of the stones is Christ. Together the cross and stones form the letter A which stands for the city of Azusa, the city in which APU is located and thrives.

The Four Cornerstones were quickly and enthusiastically approved and adopted by the Board of Trustees. All university letterheads and campus materials would use this logo. Most notably, the Four Cornerstones are beautifully highlighted at the entrance to the campus. The process and final product was a huge momentum builder for faculty and staff. It signaled a renewed future for the University.

Another major igniter came from our ten-year evaluation by the Western Association of Colleges and Universities (WASC). Our board had granted approval to the governance changes allowing faculty, staff, and student representation at board meetings, and approving reduced faculty workloads.

The faculty had rewritten the mission and purpose statement with board approval. The construction of Wilden Hall was underway and the acquisition of the west campus, Avery-Dennison, was nearly complete. The visiting WASC team found an engaged, excited and hopeful campus. We waited anxiously for the team's final report.

When the report arrived on campus, I was both floored and humbled to read, "The team strongly believes that APU can become a premier Christian, comprehensive university. It has an excellent foundation from which to transform its aspirations into reality."

This was a huge affirmation to our calling and vision for our beloved APU. To receive the affirmation of your peers who govern the WASC process brought respect and "buy in" from our entire school family.

Across campus, faculty and staff were giving each other high fives and saying, "We're on our way!" Finally after all our work, I sensed the campus community really believed we could become a Flagship university.

Four Cornerstones

President's Cabinet: Jon Wallace, Terry Franson, Pat Anderson, me, Dave Bixby, Hank Bode and Cliff Hamlow

Darling Library ribbon cutting: Paul Gray, Pat Anderson, Ted Engstrom, Richard Stack, and me

14

FINDING HOPE IN INNOVATION

"Whenever you see a successful business, someone once made a coura-geous decision."

~ Peter Drucker ~

One of our first innovative programs for the University was the introduction of an adult degree completion program. During this time adults across the nation desired to return to complete their education in record numbers. Yet, not one of the Christian colleges in California offered such programs.

Most colleges were only focused on offering typical liberal arts majors with classes offered in morning and early afternoon hours. However, working adults could not take advantage of such schedules because of their daytime jobs. With the support of our faculty leaders, we expanded into the adult bachelor's degree completion market. This was a step of faith for our undergraduate faculty steeped in the liberal arts.

There were two ways we could establish the program: either build a curriculum and delivery system from within our own faculty or acquire an established program from outside the University and work it into the cornerstones and values of APU with faculty input.

In pursuing the latter option, I soon learned of a successful Midwestern college that was closing its adult degree program. I contacted its representative and negotiated a purchase price for their entire program, lock, stock, and barrel.

Next, we needed an experienced administrator from the adult learning field. In due course, we hired an experienced and successful director, Dr. Fred Garlett, who had been a driving force in establishing a similar program in Kansas. He shared our vision that the adult market was fertile soil for APU's expansion.

Fred's first office was in a small trailer on the East Campus. He worked his way around campus, introducing himself and the degree completion concept to the rest of the faculty leaders. The business school dean, Phil Lewis, was the first to embrace the program, and he even taught the first class. Next the School of Theology adopted the adult format and was soon followed by other academic disciplines.

Our guiding emphasis for these adult programs was to keep the same spiritual focus in front of these students as the rest of the campus. Not only because *God First* was the primary cornerstone of our educational model, it's what incoming students wanted. We would be assisting these adult students in completing lifelong dreams. In many ways it enabled our faculty to see a larger field of service.

Our surveys for these new adult students revealed that the three major reasons they chose APU were our high-quality academic reputation, geographic location, and Christian values. Upon their graduation from the program over twenty-five percent of the students said the Christian values significantly impacted them. APU was a Godsend and an answer to prayer for many of these students.

We found our adult students were very serious about their studies. They were looking for meaningful take home value. They wanted real life application from the classroom to their workplace and upon completion of their degrees the opportunity to advance in their chosen professions.

A significant by-product of these programs was a financial success. The revenue from these programs allowed the university to fulfill other goals to increase faculty salaries, reduce teaching loads, and increase faculty benefits including the opportunity for our undergraduate faculty to also teach in these adult programs.

Finally, the academic centerpiece of our vision was the development of high quality doctoral programs modeled on our top-notch master's programs. This would be the ultimate step in becoming a flagship university. Already in place since 1985 was a joint doctoral program in education between APU and USC.

The Doctorate in Education seemed to be the appropriate candidate to launch our efforts. We established a Doctoral Planning Task Force in 1991 to begin our planning and development. Despite resistance by WASC and others we pressed forward.

Provost Dr. Pat Anderson and I remember the critical meeting on campus with the head of WASC, Dr. Ralph Wolf. It had been several years since his last visit and he was surprised to see the campus growth. The Ronald and Warren buildings were in place and the nearly completed Wilden Business Building had replaced the many quonset huts he remembered. The acquisition of the Avery Dennison property was nearly completed and was designated as the home for our new Doctorate in Education. Dr. Wolf noted our increase in faculty salaries, reduced teaching loads, and increasing level of faculty scholarship as favorable precursors for moving to the doctoral level.

We would finally receive approval in 1994 and award our first degrees in 1997. Today there are high quality doctoral programs in nearly every school at APU. One of the doctoral programs I foresaw as important was the Doctorate in Higher Education. As I explained to Dr. Boyer and Dr. Engstrom I imagined such a premier program would be a source of advancement for hundreds of faculty and staff throughout the one hundred and sixty institutions within the Council of Christian Colleges and Universities.

Little did I realize then the personal impact of these doctoral programs. In 2013, Dr. Amy Bragg Carey graduated from APU with an Ed.D in Higher Education. Two years later she would be appointed President at Friends University where I had previously served. It is ironic that she resides in the same President's home where I unpacked my flagship dream back in 1990 with Dr. Engstrom. How like God to move in amazing ways to bring joy and affirmation to our dreams.

On July 20, 2019 the university celebrated the 20th anniversary of Doctoral education. Dr. Laurie A. Schreiner, Chair of the

Doctoral Programs of Higher Education, delivered the keynote address followed by a panel of five alumni. The incredible growth over this period had moved the university to the status of being ranked a national university.

The vision and dreams for a flagship APU had finally come to fruition. It has been achieved due to the dedication of hundreds of faculty members over three decades. The best is yet to come.

Fred Garlett (middle), Founding Dean of the Degree Completion Program, with my daughter Melissa, and me.

15

LOST IN DARKNESS

"When wealth is lost, nothing is lost; when health is lost, something is lost; when character is lost, all is lost."

~ Billy Graham ~

t was a typical weekend, and we were busy with many commitments. That Sunday evening I was to give a speech to a group of church organizations. I had been at APU five years and my job had become not only a career but also a total lifestyle that encompasses one's life twenty-four seven.

Every waking moment is a presidential moment. The needs of the university never take a holiday. Days are filled with a wide variety of stakeholder groups that desire your time and attention. Meetings with cabinet and faculty leaders are critical. Community and church leaders request speaking times. Visibility and discourse at faculty meetings in the chapel and dining hall are important.

Attending student sports, music, and theatrical productions is essential. Evenings and weekends are frequented with valuable meetings, including board members and donors. And unexpected challenges and surprises are regularly added to my already busy agenda. God had blessed me with personal gifts to excel in my calling. I was an eager participant but did not realize the toll my job took on my personal life.

When we arrived at the venue, we entered the hall and said hello to a few people. I quickly excused myself and went into the men's bathroom. Within minutes I became dizzy, then nausea hit and I threw up. My forehead perspired and an overwhelming anxiety consumed my body and mind.

The bathroom door swung open. "Richard, what's wrong with you? Everyone is ready for you to speak right now. Are you sick?" Hearing the surprise and urgency of my wife's voice, I found the strength to get up and exit the bathroom stall. I looked up at her with a sense of defeat. I doubt she had ever seen frailty in my eyes. She looked concerned as I reached for my notes clutched in her hand.

Unsteadily, I found my way to the podium to make my remarks. Only by God's grace and will did I make it through the presentation. This frightening experience forced me to admit that my world had become overwhelming, and that I was merely surviving, not thriving.

Like Carl Sandberg's proverbial fog, my burnout crept in slowly "on little cat feet." Throughout my life, personal qualities made me a most unlikely candidate for depression or burnout. Hope, boundless energy, optimism, and passion had always made a difference and fortified the core of my being.

My dreams were usually inspiring, and I flew effortlessly through the air with the utmost of ease. Nothing was beyond my ability to achieve. As the ultimate high-achiever, the lure of tackling any challenge was high and my need for sleep and rest low. But now only nightmares came to me at night.

I should have seen the warning signs of my impending depression. I was often tired, more agitated than usual, drinking way more coffee than I cared to admit, and my dreams haunted me at night. I became afraid of tomorrow.

In the haze of   morning the next day after my speech, I awoke upon hearing the door close as Vivian left for work at the university. I bent over on the edge of my bed and wondered, *Was this what depression felt like? Would I lose my ability to lead? Was this the end of my calling? Oh God, help me!*

I tried to stand up, but fell to the floor and felt as though I was drowning in my uncontrollable tears of pain. I lay on my back with eyes closed, and the truth of what was happening broke through to my rational mind.

I saw the unending parade of events which had taken a toll on my body and soul, my children leaving home for college and three major moves to three different states. I lost the immediate proximity to my long-time YPO support group and other friends. I was in a serious bicycle accident that deprived me of pursuing one of my favorite sports and much needed exercise. I no longer made time to hike, and I was drinking buckets of caffeine from the coffee machine.

This reflective reality check began a long road of unyielding desperation. It made me realize the obvious; I had failed to slow down and make time to nurture my body and soul. I allowed myself to become stretched too far emotionally, physically, and spiritually. I had always guided other leaders with the axiom *Give Your Best, But Not Your All.* I stopped following my advice and key commandment.

In reflection, these personal qualities were significant, natural precursors in my calling as a university president, but I needed to balance my time with their time. As you discovered in this book, our first five years at APU had been exciting and rewarding. However, in the midst of the school's incredible growth and success, I failed to slow down to recharge. And finally, the thread that bound my soul broke.

For the following weeks, my outlook darkened, my confidence dimmed and the joy I once felt faded away. In contrast to my previous energy-fired daily enthusiasm, I now pleaded with God to bring restoration and give me the strength to just live, let alone lead the university.

In my unfamiliar reality, I cancelled appointments and refused invitations, even rescinded on a major mission trip to Africa that coming summer. Relationships, both with family and professional, had become taxing rather than stimulating. I retreated to a self-imposed island where I alone lived, abandoned and in despair.

Perhaps the worst part of all, some of my colleagues took notice and expressed concern regarding my uncertainty and lack of enthusiasm. Vivian asked me again and again if I was ill. The answer to each inquiry was to tell them I was just tired, but otherwise okay. It saddened me to know that this was not true, but how could I share the truth? My head swam with more questions than answers during this period.

There was no miracle, no medical cure that brought an end to my four months of desperation. In actuality, prayer, gratitude, and conversations with God set the reset button. During these dialogues, I filled my soul with my life verse: "Jesus Christ, the same yesterday, today, and forever." Hebrews 13:8

God used my memory to reflect on my challenging past when my Grandmother Grace rescued me and she taught to love and trust Jesus. Through early disappointments in my childhood, God was always there, leading me to become a resilient person with an unswerving faith in His promises. I had been blessed. My teachers and pastor steered me toward a college education where I became mature in my faith, yet now I was a missing sheep who had lost his way.

Despite the fact that my current burnout was unfamiliar territory for me, it reminded me that God loved me now just as he had in the yesterdays of my life.

I began thanking him for his calling on my life, and with humility and gratitude, my restoration began. The passage "In everything, give thanks..." Thessalonians 5:18 brought new meaning to my transformation. As something I read once said, *a person's difficulties end when gratitude begins.*

During this time of healing, I also replaced my coffee addiction with regular hikes up the Garcia Trail where I found much needed peace and rest for my soul. The first day I hiked to the top of the trail, I noticed a large letter "A" that can be seen throughout much of the San Gabriel Valley. Over the years the "A" in the formation had been damaged by high winds or fire, but new generations of students always found a way to rebuild and repair it.

Each day I hiked, I grew stronger as I navigated the rocky path surrounded by burned out grass. I was better equipped with prayers of gratitude regularly, and these hikes gave deep spiritual value to me.

It is significant to note that several years prior a mountain fire in the San Gabriel Valley scorched the earth and left nothing behind but ashes. A forbidding black expanse replaced the beautiful lush mountainside for months. But now on my hikes, I marveled at the beautiful plants and wildflowers that lined the trail, a miracle of sorts.

Local scientists reported that some fresh growth comprised plant varieties that had not been seen in over a hundred years. Just as God transformed the mountain and made it more magnificent than ever, he also transformed me from the dark lifeless ashes of four months to a rebirth that brought more joy, confidence, and renewed purpose back into my life.

Never again would I take this miracle of healing for granted. I rededicated myself to follow the lead of my heavenly Father to lead APU: Yesterday, Tomorrow, and Forever.

JESUS CHRIST IS THE SAME YESTERDAY AND TODAY AND FOREVER. HEBREWS 13:8

My Life Verse

PART FOUR
COMMITMENT TO SERVICE

16

MIRACLES AND LOSS

"Be strong and courageous. Do not be afraid or terrified because of them, for the Lord your God goes with you; he will never leave you nor forsake you."

~ Deuteronomy 31:6 ~

I can remember a dreadful day in January 1997 when my wife Vivian drove into our driveway at Foxglove Court and slumped over the steering wheel with tears streaming down her face. The doctor had diagnosed her with incurable breast cancer. I opened the car door and her eyes expressed anguish as her voice broke with the terrible news.

I knelt down and wiped the tears and hair away from her face. I lifted her out of the car and carried her into our home. My life would never be the same from that moment forward. It was a tough year for our family as we battled her cancer and our fear.

In November of that same year, I was involved in a bike accident on the Pacific Coast Highway. I had lost control of my bike and suffered severe facial lacerations and a concussion that left me unconscious for hours before I woke up in the Mission Viejo Hospital.

Early the next morning I was doing my devotions in the hospital bed when I fell into a dream state in which I was hovering over a beautiful field of flowers. I was floating gently with a waft of fragrant breezes in the air. I could hear the faint sound of a sheep bleating in the distance where I glided slowly. Soon I approached the edge of a steep cliff that dropped to the ocean. I saw the bleating sheep on a tree branch just below the cliff's edge. I realized in that moment that I was the sheep. I had come close to death, only to be saved by the hand of God.

I awoke with tears streaming down my face and noticed the droplets on my Bible. Rays of light made their way through the hospital room's windows, shining on me and I knew it was God showing me His love in a tangible, physical way. I knew that He truly cared for me; He was my shepherd, and I was His valued sheep.

During Vivian's battle with cancer, I often recalled that instant when God saved my life. It was that miracle that kept my hope alive, that she would ultimately be saved as well.

Vivian's impact on APU was expansive and fruitful. From the very beginning of our time there, she was visible and available across campus to students, faculty, and staff. She led a mentoring program for a dozen or more women and staff on campus who became known as her Dream Team.

Each year she would select four female students, recommended by campus leaders, to mentor on a weekly basis. Often they would be at our home enjoying an evening meal with our family. A few times they spent a weekend in retreat off campus. Our Thanksgiving always found a group of international students sharing our traditional turkey and other delights.

She was even a force for the school in the realm of fundraising. For example, she planned and organized the first Foundations program for the Advancement Office. Because of these efforts, APU for the first time received six- and seven-figure gifts from Southern California foundations such as Fletcher Jones; often major leadership gifts to our several new buildings on campus.

After her death, her journals revealed she had been praying for a new ministry just months before they diagnosed her with cancer. She had resigned from her foundation position, passing along her prayers for a new ministry on campus. But once she learned her cancer was terminal with no known cure, she thanked God that her new ministry was to die for Him. She told me to pray for a miracle while she herself moved into the school of dying graces.

She shared openly through campus emails her journey with The Beast, her name for the cancer. She shared both her pain and the lessons she was learning, wanting to be transparent to the entire campus community as part of her ministry.

She asked our campus pastor, Lawrence Witherspoon, to conduct a healing service on campus; she felt God wanted this service, not for herself, but for those on campus needing special healing. At least two students with forms of blood diseases were healed that day.

You will never know how much you really love someone until you watch them in the crucible of dying. Her faith and trust in God was inspiring to all of us. She loved to celebrate the promises in God's word by repeating them. During those last two years, I fell in love with my wife at a level I never imagined.

The summer and fall semesters following her death were difficult. I needed to recover from almost total exhaustion, not realizing until then I had been operating on little to no physical reserves and I needed rest.

I also wanted the support of my family, and I desired to spend time with them. We all needed to share our grief together, reflecting upon our family's journey with Vivian, and the wonderful life God had given us together.

On a professional level, it was necessary to examine my vocation versus my calling. Vivian and I had been a team. Now my teammate was no longer by my side. I needed to discover God's will for my future. I wanted to return to serve the APU community and continue the calling we had received from God a decade earlier. I wanted to fulfill my promise to Vivian to finish well. I still missed her deeply, and there were moments I had difficulty believing she was not around.

As I have grown older and wiser, it has become clear that my destiny has been a lot about overcoming difficulties, disappointments, abandonments, roadblocks, and other obstacles of life. It appears that the purpose for my struggles was part of a much larger plan to make me the person God intended me to be.

Maybe this is what Max DePree meant in Leadership Jazz when he wrote, "Leaders need to learn not to inflict pain, but to bear pain. If you're bearing pain properly as a leader, whether you're a preacher, a college professor, a parent or a teacher, you ought to bear the marks of the struggle. One ought to have bruised shins and skinned knees."

Inside I knew I had unswervingly pledged my allegiance to God's promises no matter how difficult the circumstances. Christ had been my ultimate example. How could I expect any less for myself.

During our last few years of my presidency, the Advancement team, led by Dr. Dave Bixby, had been working hard on the Going Beyond fundraising campaign, to great success. After congratulating everyone involved on its successful completion, I had one last request. Considering the upcoming Centennial, wouldn't it be wonderful to complete the one project left unfunded in our campaign, the event center? It would be a multi-purpose building, accommodating not only athletic events but also serving as the West Campus chapel site, commencement ceremonies location and host to many community activities.

I challenged the board to help us contact our top fifteen donor prospects to consider leadership gifts for the event center, to mobilize their network of contacts, and consider making another major gift themselves. If we could generate at least fifty percent of the building's cost, we might launch a wider fundraising effort with our friends.

We all prayed for continued support for the event center, realizing we had just completed a twenty million dollar campaign. Dr. Bixby recalled my speaking in chapel and saying to the student body, "If you have any grandparents or parents that would come alongside the university and help with a lead gift for the event center, the board could move ahead with the project."

That next day a student called Dave's office and said we should call on his grandfather who served on a local foundation. The student's mother and Dave made an appointment and visited with Mr. George Koeberle of the Gunther Foundation. Three months later the Foundation made a three million dollar lead gift commitment to the APU event center.

After sharing this pledge with our board of trustees and the ongoing excitement that ensued, we had to figure out from where the remainder of the funds would be raised. This initial pledge covered approximately one-third of the total anticipated cost. Where would the remaining funds come from?

One board member wondered whether we could honestly accept the gift if we wouldn't be able to raise the additional funds for at least another five years. Another board member said that I, as president, would need to dedicate myself full-time to raising those dollars, but given Vivian's cancer progression how might I devote myself to such a task. The board waited until our fall board meeting to decide whether we could accept this gift in good faith.

After the meeting, Dr. Ted Engstrom said to me, "Even though the timing doesn't seem to be right, I believe God is in this gift. I suggest you and I pray the five loaves and two fishes prayer." We both prayed daily.

Several sizable new pledges and gifts were miraculously in hand by our next board meeting in the fall, bringing the percentage of funds needed for construction to nearly fifty percent. The board decided to move ahead with accepting the leadership gifts and allowing the Administration to work toward securing the remaining amount.

During this period, Vivian was hospitalized at the City of Hope and in treatment. She was not doing well. I was trying my best to lead the University and care for my wife. Then a miracle happened and one of our prayers was answered. Dave Bixby and I were invited to the Hugh and Hazel Darling Foundation in Los Angeles to meet with Mr. Stack. It was a great visit, and the Foundation committed one million dollars to the Event Center project. We were so happy and high-fived all the way home until my personal reality crept in. About thirty minutes into our drive, I asked Dave to drop me off at the City of Hope.

He remembered my countenance changed immediately. On one hand we celebrated the million-dollar gift, but on the other we realized the most important things in life are not about money or success. It's about how you love and how you treat those closest to you. And we were all praying for another miracle with Vivian. Unfortunately, a little over one year later the arms of Jesus embraced my beloved wife Vivian. During that first summer after her parting, my heart walked each day to the gate of our love and waited for her return. And each day I told my soul that she would never return, that she had died and gone to be with Jesus. At the time my soul had trouble understanding and dealing with the pain, but I would come to realize my heart would eventually heal. Only time and God's grace would help me through the journey to recovery. It was a tough time for all of us, and we would learn the hard lesson that only time heals the pain of loss and letting go of the ones we love.

Dedication of the Vivian Felix Healing Garden

THE
SCHOOL OF DYING GRACES

*Lessons on living
from two extraordinary
journeys toward God*

RICHARD FELIX
WITH ROB WILKINS

❧ FOREWORDS BY ❧
RICHARD FOSTER AND JACK HAYFORD

17

CONTEMPLATION AND LETTING GO

"The time is always right to do what is right."

~ Martin Luther King Jr. ~

After Vivian's death, I realized my time as President was coming to an end. As I considered and prayed about what might be the best time to retire, I thought back to the closing night of the 1992 Barcelona Olympics.

I sat in that great stadium amongst 80,000 people next to APU's track and field coach, Terry Franson. I looked at him and said, "Terry, you must be proud to have seven of your world-class athletes competing tonight on the world's greatest stage."

He raised his eyebrows and shook his head in disbelief, "Richard, I am humbled and so proud of each of them and their triumphant stories. I'm even more grateful that they are disciples of Jesus Christ and competing for his glory."

On this special closing night our seven APU Olympic athletes would earn five medals, more than many other competing nations.

Mike Barnett finished 7th in the javelin. It was the highest finish in that event by an American in over four decades. Kris Akabusi earned silver medals in the 400 hurdles and the 4 x 400-relay representing Great Britain. Decathlete David Johnson, despite a broken bone in his foot, finished with the bronze medal. Our other two Olympians were Innocent Egbunike and Ben Koech.

Two of our students, Davidson and Osmond Ezinwa, the fastest twins in the world, led the Nigerian 4 x 400-relay team to a silver medal. They finished second because of one slow hand off. I remain fascinated with the coordination and teamwork needed to negotiate passing the baton while running at breakneck speed.

The timing to pass off the baton is an analogous concept of letting go. People offer much literature on the Christian idea of a person's *calling*, but very little when you are *uncalled*.

Nothing lasts forever. There is a beginning and an end to every assignment, venture, project or career. We place so much attention and emphasis on our beginnings and maintaining our stamina after we start, but very little on how we will conclude our own race.

Maybe because of our culture's emphasis on striving and chasing success, I've often noticed that leaders give very little time and thought to the completion of their particular venture. So they continue to hang on to their calling—it becomes part of who they are, and letting go means losing their identity, their reason to live. They do not know how to pass the baton, to give someone else the glory. This stubbornness too often causes their organizations to atrophy.

My mentors taught me that sensing God's leading and direction to complete one's calling is of great importance. I'm a firm believer in the Biblical command to *finish well*. I believe that finishing well means knowing when you have been uncalled. "I've fought a good fight, have finished my course and have kept the faith." 2 Timothy 4:7.

During my last year as president of APU, I had a recurring dream of climbing a mountain with my administrative team. Each time we reached the summit, another rose even higher just ahead of us. I encouraged my team to go on without me because I needed to rest, so they packed up and left for the summit.

I experienced a sense of relief when I saw them climb the mountain without me. And then my dream ended. I understood not every dream has a meaning, but this one did. It was a vivid and recurring vision that stuck with me for days afterward.

When dreams are recurrent, it sometimes suggests that there's an issue or problem you have yet to resolve. I interpreted this as my need to decide if I should continue my presidency. So, being of a bit of a mystic, I paid attention to this one. Perhaps God was sending me a message, and my time at APU appeared to be ending.

After twenty-one years of loving my work and performing the tasks of a university president, I admitted the job itself was no longer as engaging as it once was. Vivian was no longer by my side. We were a team, a four-legged table that held up the weight of the world together and now I was trying my best to stand on two legs. I was changing, not only professionally, but personally. I did not look at my life in the same perspective—it was no longer about doing, but about being. I felt there were other shorter races I could run for God that would help to grow His kingdom for the future.

The time for me finally came to hand off the baton of leadership to someone else at my beloved APU. So I asked the board for a short sabbatical away from my responsibilities in January and February 2000. I needed time to rest, pray, and ask God for a sense of assurance that this was the direction he wanted for my life.

During this time away, my heart and ego's struggle began, and then intensified. The more that I prayed about staying at APU, the more I realized that God was whispering to let go.

I sensed a peace in my inner being as each day passed. But occasionally my ego reared its ugly head and shouted out, "No, no, Richard! This is your dream job and you can't let go of it!" But a still small voice whispered again and again, assuring me it was okay to surrender my position.

I must confess there were moments my ego stoked my vanity by saying, "But I like being president of a university. I take pride in the prestige and thrive in the power."

God's voice whispered again, "It's time to relinquish your duties". Then my ego changed its tactics and used the pain of loss I felt against me. "Listen, your APU community will give you a bounty of sympathy for years to come. All will be well."

For several weeks the skirmish between God's voice and my ego battled, which startled me because I thought I had let go of that ego thing a long time ago. I was glad when my God's mighty word won the last match.

I could have delayed this decision for another year or two, but that would deny God's direction. Equally important was the fact that important things were in store for APU that suggested it seemed like the right time for a leadership change.

First, a new five-year strategic plan needed to be put in place and a feasibility study to prepare for our next comprehensive fundraising campaign that would catapult APU to an extra level of leadership and advancement of God's kingdom. Pulling off the plan successfully would require a strong presidential vision and a three to five year commitment, neither of which I was prepared to complete.

Second, the next strategic visit for WASC was planned for March 2001. A new president needed to be in place to present the University's vision for the future to continue APU's commitment to excellence. Delaying my departure would not benefit this process.

As I reflected on my decade of leadership at APU, I realized we had met almost every one of the goals laid out in my inaugural address. Enrollment exploded. A second campus and several recent buildings dotted the landscape. The adult and graduate offerings including the doctoral programs were successful. We reduced faculty loads and increased their salaries significantly. And new scholarships flourished at all levels.

In addition, a stronger faculty emerged and was to oversee the university governance. We built an outstanding, generous and committed board of trustees. Our donor base expanded exponentially. APU moved full steam ahead on the sea of higher education. Most importantly, the spiritual life on campus had never been more vibrant. Students and faculty fully embraced the *God First* ethos. First-time visitors to campus felt the powerful spirit of place, the unique culture shaped by the four cornerstones.

Azusa Pacific achieved everything I had envisioned a flagship Christian university to be way back when it was just a dream in Kansas along the Yellow Brick Road. The APU enrollment in 1989 was around 2100 students and it operated on a budget of $22 million. Later in 2000 when I resigned, the student enrollment had grown to 6,125 students; the budget had increased to $83 million and the student retention rate went from 48% to 82%.

I felt confident the leadership transition would go smoothly, and the university would not miss a beat and the momentum would continue without my daily presence. The board would not select a new president who didn't share the ideals we worked so hard to carry out the previous ten years. I knew that successful organizations hired new leaders from within while struggling institutions hired from the outside. Although I would not be involved in the selection process, I felt confident the board shared my beliefs and I could at least help pave the way. I reasoned there would be a flawless handoff of the baton to my most valued teammate, Jon Wallace.

Early on I asked Jon to be my second-in-command during Vivian's illness. This decision would be the silver lining during that tough time and end up benefiting the University. In my prolonged absence, Jon's leadership emerged, as did our community's acceptance of his guidance and direction. It soon became clear that my team would follow Jon anywhere. Not only did they trust him, but also Jon's love for the students was unequalled. His passion to fulfill the great commission through higher education made him a natural person to lead APU. In many ways, Jon was a mentor to me, as much as I had been to him.

Davidson and Osmond Ezinwa, Silver Medalists at the Barcelona Olympics with coach Terry Franson and me

With Dr. Jon Wallace, my First Mate on the APU Flagship

18

GRACE AND REFLECTION IN RETIREMENT

"There is no greater love than to lay down one's life for others."

~ John 15:13 ~

At the end of my last board meeting, which occurred in May 2000, the Chairman asked me to leave the room so the board could go into executive session. I did not understand what was happening. In prior times I had always been informed ahead of time when they needed to go into executive session. It puzzled me. It couldn't be about my performance because I was retiring in less than sixty days.

A short time later, I reentered the room, and they asked me to remain standing. What in the world was going on? The Chairman asked someone to open the door of the closed bulletin board and to my shock, I saw a sketch of the new APU event's building with a sign hanging on the building that read, The Richard and Vivian Felix Event Center.

The Chairman read the buildings' name aloud, the entire board stood and applauded. I was speechless. The tears flowed from my eyes and I tried to smile, but my heart sank as I thought about my dear Vivian who was not here with me to celebrate this honor.

I remarked to the group that perhaps they needed to rethink their decision because only dead and rich people have their names placed on buildings, and I hadn't succumbed to either of those scenarios yet.

One of the board members joked that the board originally wanted to put only Vivian's name on the building but then thought perhaps I might want to share the billing with her. Everyone laughed and gathered around. A few members asked, "Maybe we can get you to reconsider your decision to retire now?"

I smiled at them with confidence, knowing it was the right time to depart. I had given it my best. I expressed my sincere gratitude for a decade of service, took my final bow, and gave my last curtain call as the president of Azusa Pacific University.

Now, each time I return to campus, I make my way to the upper plaza on the west campus to have a moment of prayer at the Vivian Felix Healing Garden. Bill Catling's angel statue reminds us, "She is not here, but she has risen to be with Jesus." Remembering her time of ministry on campus brings me great pleasure.

All the pieces of my future prospects became clear as I began my retirement. I had more time to renew my intentions and goals for the next few years. I would spend more time with my family, and take much needed time to complete her memoir, *The School of Dying Graces.*

In the book, I wrote about my experience of losing Vivian and the healing process after her death. Since its publication, I have received hundreds of cards, emails, and letters from members of our campus community talking about changes they had made in their own lives because of Vivian's incredible faith and devotion to God. Her impact will forever influence the APU community.

Letting go of my presidency was difficult to do, but God's timing was perfect. At my final board meeting, I offered five major challenges that would face our beloved APU in the years ahead.

The first challenge I believed to be the most crucial was to keep the motto *God First*. We don't want our graduates to go the way of our nation's first institution of higher education, Harvard. Within a thirty-minute drive of our campus, there are at least three other colleges who had also started with a *God First* maxim, but who now have other priorities guiding their halls of learning. We don't want to go down that road, but remain diligent and faithful.

The second challenge was to balance a strong undergraduate liberal arts curriculum with the adult and graduate programs. We must never sacrifice the basic commitment to the liberal arts no matter the circumstances, because the undergraduate students are the lifeblood, the core purpose of APU's existence. So balance is key.

The third challenge was financial. For the first seventy-five years of the University's history, the leaders had struggled to balance budgets and find the resources to fund their dreams. Such needs resulted in an extraordinary faith in God to provide the resources, which He did. While the University was now stronger financially than it ever had been before, it must not lesson our dependence and hope on God; rather it must always place Him first in all financial decisions, in how to best establish an endowment for the future.

The fourth challenge was to preserve the entrepreneurial, risk-taking philosophy that had been APU's hallmark. The University has always had a culture that values fresh ideas, not toxic dissent and the easy comfort of familiarity to ensnare the unwary. Therefore, APU must resist efforts to move to a status quo, a stationary environment.

The fifth challenge would be to keep up with technological changes that happens almost by the hour. Technology itself is neither good nor bad, but how it's used is never neutral. The University must be able to adapt to technology's ever-changing influence on our strategic purposes, while keeping *God First*.

All the accomplishments during our tenure can be interpreted as *God Moments*. It is important to understand our planning was due to great human effort but during so many of our successes we would look at each other and say, "Surely this was a God Moment." Again and again collectively we witnessed the divine intervene at the appointed moments. We were blessed to enjoy ten seasons of sacred moments together.

After I retired, I found it gratifying, yet humbling to read the Time Magazine article from February 2, 2004, the thrust of which shared that "Christian colleges are booming—and reinventing the meaning of faith-based education." The article referred to APU as a leader in this renaissance and used our campus as the prototype of a leading edge type of university. I read the article again, smiled, then said out loud, "Thank you, Lord." Azusa Pacific had become a flagship university.

I also could have never imagined that in 2005 I'd receive an unexpected invitation from Jefferson High School in Indiana. My Alma Mater informed me they had elected me to its Hall of Fame. Who knew? Wouldn't my teachers and classmates be surprised to see the enormous bright white smile on my face? I felt proud of that abandoned child who had been rescued by his Grandmother Grace and later by Christ, who was recognized by his high school for his life's work that was devoted to Christ, Scholarship, Community, and Service.

And thus ends my story of a rejected little boy from a small town in Indiana, who grew into a man who was nothing like his father on earth, but hopefully more like his father in heaven. My hope is that I put to good use the token of faith my church community bestowed upon me to do *good works* in our blessed and beautiful world.

ACKNOWLEDGMENTS

"Kind words can be short and easy to speak, but their echoes are endless."

~ Mother Teresa ~

Every life lesson in this memoir is attributable to hundreds of mentors who touched me along my journey. Teachers, pastors, university colleagues, board members, benefactors, and especially those wonderful college students—you know who you are—I wish I could list each one of you. Thank you so much for speaking faith into my life.

My family means everything to me. My wife, Susan, is a constant cheerleader and encourager who assisted in the completion of this project. She is my angel here on earth. My wonderful family has always been a joy to me over the years - Doak, Tristram and Amy, Melissa and Lance, who have lived blessed and meaningful lives. They are a testament to God's goodness in life. A big hug to my five wonderful grandchildren: Tatum Marshall, Collier Marshall, Jackson Felix, Benjamin Felix, and Lily Felix. And with heartfelt appreciation to my grandmother Grace Penrod who took care of me and to Aunt Maxine Young who was like a second mom in my life.

A special note of gratitude to my writer Marta M. Mobley, a gracious writing coach, critic, and champion who helped me to put all my life pieces into the right place. I also wish to thank Story Terrace staff for their guidance throughout the process.

Richard and Vivian Felix Event Center

Family Picture in Retirement

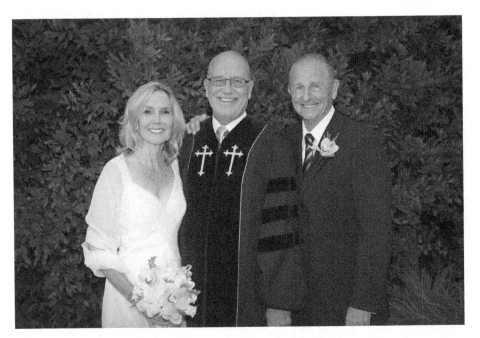

Marriage to Susan in 2009 by our friend Gordon Kirk

If you have any comments or questions please email
atokenoffaith@gmail.com

Story Terrace

Made in the USA
Middletown, DE
06 November 2020